PRACTICAL BRITISH
LIGHTWEIGHT TWO-STROKE
MOTORCYCLES

Foulis

Haynes
®

STEVE WILSON

ISBN 0 85429 709 X

A FOULIS Motorcycling book

First published May 1990
© Steve Wilson 1990

Published by:
Haynes Publishing Group
Sparkford, Near Yeovil, Somerset.
BA22 7JJ, England

Haynes Publications Inc
861 Lawrence Drive, Newbury Park
California 91320 USA

British Library Cataloguing in Publication Data
Wilson, Steve, *1943–*
    Practical British two-stroke lightweight motorcycles.
    1. British two–stroke lightweight motorcycles
    I. Title
    629.2'275

    ISBN 0-85429-709-X

Library of Congress catalog card number
89-81506

Editor: **Jeff Clew**
Page Layout: **Mike King**
Printed in England by: **J.H. Haynes & Co. Ltd.**

The cover illustration shows a 1961 Norman B4 Sports Twin fitted with a Villiers 2T 250cc twin cylinder engine.

Contents

Acknowledgements

For their assistance the author would like to thank Owen Wright of the BSA Owners Club, Peggy and Rowland Carter of the Bantam Owners and Andy Tidball of T and G, all for help with the Bantam chapter.

For the Villiers engine machines it's thanks (again) to Nick Kelly of the British Two Stroke Club. For the photographs, grateful thanks to Cyril Ayton at *Motorcycle Sport,* and also to Kim White at the EMAP Archives for her assistance. I must add unbounded admiration for the flying fingers of ace typist Sandra den Hertog on this short order; and finally express sincere gratitude for both the patience and the practical assistance of my editor and fellow author, Jeff Clew.

The camel died, the Bantam didn't. British lightweights really can be pracitical, as this D1 outfit in the desert proves.

Chapter One
What this book is about

This book is about love and money. It's for those who feel the former, but lack the latter.

It does hope to show that some British lightweights can make practical mounts for economical everyday transport, but it would be a blinkered runner indeed who did not recognise and admit that modern Japanese and East European lightweights already offer very viable, ready-made economy two-wheeled transport, just as cheap, better equipped, with equal or better performance, and usually a great deal more convenient. With step-throughs and MZs available, why bother with a Bantam?

'Why?' is indeed a question you may ask yourself with varying degrees of emphasis as your James's electrics let you down on the ride to work for the third time in a week, or your Bantam's gearchange return spring breaks again (meaning a crankcase split to replace it). With so many practical deterrents, it has to be a love job.

Just why you should feel drawn to the ancient Brits is another matter, and probably as imponderable a question in its way as the one from the girl who asked a jazz musician what rhythm was, to which he replied 'Lady, if you ain't got it, I can't tell you'. To most, British iron means the road to danger, insolvency, social opprobrium and a lifetime of dirty fingernails, and British lightweights mean all that without even the compensation of some speed and charisma. Now to my mind some lightweights do have style, even if it sometimes embodies a kind of inverted snobbery — beside a well-used Francis-Barnett with its all-over Arden Green finish reduced by years of road dirt to a patina of filth, an MZ is a Maserati. No, the only real explanation is a fatal attraction — but mixed in with a dash of low cunning. If you follow the few simple rules in this tome, with luck you not only won't lose any money but, in addition to the inestimable character building which the process of keeping an ancient Brit running brings with it, you might actually come out a little way ahead.

Which brings us back to money. In some ways this book has come about because of market forces. The cost of buying and owning a genuine classic British motorcycle, in the dictionary definition of 'classic' as 'of the first rank', has become beyond the reach of most of us; Manx Nortons or Vincent twins are now fetching well over £10,000. Partly this is due to genuine recognition of these machines' fine quality, and partly to more material considerations. While under Britain's capital transfer tax law, works of art are classed as taxable assets, old vehicles in general are not, and so the wealthy have discovered a way of investing money without a tax penalty and one which, given the machines' steadily rising prices, also represents a hedge against inflation.

The BSA Bantam and other British lightweights opened up many possibilities, as this lovely publicity picture suggests. Write your own caption.

With a knock-on effect, usage of the word 'classic' has been optimistically expanded to include 'obsolete' (in trade terms, anything manufactured for the last time over ten years previously), or just plain old. So the price of worthwhile but ordinary post-war roadsters has also risen sharply. Already we are regularly seeing the £2000 BSA A10 650 twin, the £1500 Matchless 350cc single.

So, for young people keen to get involved in the old bike scene, for the enthusiast of limited means, perhaps returning to motorcycling once their family has grown up, or for the rider with a 'classic' which is now too good (and valuable, and vulnerable) to risk on the daily ride to work, it's time to consider the British lightweight. The above three categories of person are broadly the ones this book will be aimed at, so some of it will be old news to some readers. A seasoned rider will not need the bits of advice on assembling a tool kit etc, but I feel a duty to also aim at the individual most of us were to begin with — young, with little money, and not much of a clue. Even to an expert, the machine sections may be a useful reminder, 6 and with new regulations and laws, and the scene changing all the time, much of the general information should be useful to the born-again rider.

So let us consider the British Industry's post-war utility models, the low performance ones previously dismissed by speed merchants and boy racers with an affectionately contemptuous epithet — 'grey porridge'!

Chapter Two

The reason why
and the basic guidelines

As stated, a cocktail of love and money is the motive force for running a British lightweight, but in the course of doing so, you may have to argue the case a little more logically — to your parents if you're still living at home, to a partner, to the bank manager if a small loan or overdraft is involved, or even, when the going gets rough, to yourself.

First, unlike a modern machine, there will be no depreciation, and if you don't spend more on restoration than you can get for your machine when you dispose of it, you are unlikely to lose money. Restoration is an activity dear to many, with its own skills and rewards, but as the 'Practical' part of this book's title indicates, it is not our primary concern. Some of the information that follows may assist in it, but the attitude of rigid adherence to the original spec. and finish can discourage you from actually using the bike, as well as bumping up the budget. Where modern improvements exist, they will be detailed.

Second, the selected machines are cheap to run, all offering at least 60 miles to the gallon. Spares are cheap and for the important bit, the engines, almost universally available. These bikes are also cheaper than larger ones to tax, and there are tailor-made low-cost insurance schemes available, which we will detail.

Thirdly, while in no way performance motorcycles, these machines were built to last. While it would be idle to deny that Oriental lightweights can offer long service too, comments made by Geoff Duke after a visit to Japan at the beginning of the 60s are indicative of a different basic approach. 'From enquiries I made,' he wrote, 'the average life of a Japanese motorcycle was 25,000 to 30,000 miles. One must take into account, though, the fact that most Japanese owners change their motorcycles at yearly intervals . . . and during this period seem to give them little or no attention.' This throwaway philosophy was in contrast to the make-do-and-mend tradition over here.

Furthermore, the selected machines were the culmination of long

Early days - 50,000 Bantams built by 1950, and another twenty years production lay ahead.

evolution and production runs; development and increased reliability may not have been applied in a smooth progression during that time, but in the end it was often attained. Around half a million Bantams were built, and their use by the GPO for telegram deliveries, for which the late B175s were included, by its nature an urgent job, indicates their trustworthiness. By 1960, no less than 2½ million engine units had been produced by Villiers of Wolverhampton, and though a large proportion were for industrial applications, over 1 million had been motorcycle engines; the simplicity of design, reliable assembly standards, and reasonably efficient electrics of the late 197cc 9E singles and their derivatives, and of the

Following page: *'Cock o' the Lightweights', by 1953 the Bantam was showing its appeal to both sexes and all ages. The same is true today.*

P. Thomas, on a Surrey, on B.S.A. Bantam with P. Beggs, who as pillion passenger went recently on a 4,500 miles European tour.

Mr. W. Payne, 1,158 - mile trip from Adelaide to Lake Eyre, Australia, on a B.S.A. Bantam. Fuel consumption averaged 136 m.p.g.

Mr. and Mrs. C. Shorney, of Middlesex, England, on their B.S.A. Bantam, on which they travelled 2,060 miles to Austria and back.

Gerald O. Wills has covered 6,355 miles on a tour through seven European countries on his B.S.A. Bantam. Average fuel consumption 135 m.p.g.

Mrs. Clara Keer, a 75-year-old grandmother, of Wexham, Bucks, England, is a proud possessor of a B.S.A. Bantam.

Mr. W. L. Rawson, M.B.E., with Mr. G. Earl, a B.S.A. Bantam owner, before he undertook a 4,000 mile trip.

Travel To the

**BSA
BANTAM
125 c.c.**

OVER 70,000 RIDERS ALL OVER THE

...ning her after ob-
...ng licence, Nurse Joy
...McKean toured 4,205
...iles on her Bantam
...r a fuel cost of
...ss than £6.

Mr. Wm. Lane, 82 years
old, who recently rode
from Land's End to
John O'Groats in six
days on his Bantam.

Three Adelaide nurses—
Juliet Jennings, Ann Bick-
more and Mattie Lamont
(L to R) with their Bantams
on which they toured Tas-
mania, New Zealand and
Australia.

sted
uughout
the World

Members of the 70-
strong London Bantam
Motor Cycle Club
setting out on their Con-
tinental "Over the Alps"
tour.

Councillor T. Neville, of
Tansley, Derbyshire, a
73-years-old Bantam
enthusiast.

Mr. C. Morris, of
Victoria Park, West-
ern Australia, who
recently completed
a 4,030 mile trip on
a B.S.A. Bantam,
his first machine.

BSA 125

...ORLD ARE USING B.S.A. BANTAMS

2T 250 twin cylinder engines, were widely recognised. If the quest for performance is set aside, some of the machines they powered represent potentially excellent utility mounts.

Performance, in fact, is one part of the formula to which this book is written, which is: 50mph, and £500. A 175 Bantam in 1968 saw 64mph, a 9E-engined Ambassador T3 Star in 1960 gave 55mph and any 2T-engined machine, Leader or Arrow was good for around 70mph. Even allowing for age, the half-ton is still just attainable for all the above models, and that seems to me to be the practical minimum for use in an era where, as one 125 Bantam D1 rider put it to me glumly, 'Even the traffic jams move at 30mph!'

£500 may sound a lot for an old lightweight, so let's be specific; that sum is not just the purchase price of the machine, but the total budget, with the only exclusions being licences, road tax, test and training fees, i.e. it's intended to cover buying the bike, necessary work on it, clothing and equipment, MOT and insurance. (The exception is the Ariel Leader/Arrow, where higher prices mean that the budget is really only likely to cover the machine itself; this will be discussed further in Chapter 10.) Otherwise there will be other ongoing expenses and uprating, but the £500 should see you on the road, legally and in good order. That's my idea of 'Practical'. People will tell you about doing it for less, but they will turn out to have had a head start in terms of equipment, contacts or skills, and to have failed to take into account 'hidden' items like the cost of phone calls, postage and travelling to shops or autojumbles. This is the basic budget for beginners. It is fluid — some items you may have already, which gives you more to play with elsewhere. Just one final general word: in this world, unfortunately nothing is for nothing, and if you are not in a position to set aside that sum, then enjoy the book but forget about doing it, because otherwise grief and frustration will almost certainly follow.

Chapter Three
What this book will not do

Having defined what this book will try to do - tell you how you can achieve some individual, potentially reliable transport with reasonable performance, on a budget - it's time to say what it won't do.

It will not provide a full history of the marques involved or, in some cases not even a detailed year-by-year development history of the models, as in the case of the many Villiers-engined models, space does not permit this. But by book lists and other suggestions, it will indicate where you can find that information when you need it.

It will not tell you how to make these machines go faster. There were trials and scrambles versions of the Villiers singles, and the Bantam Racing Club has been a well-respected entrance to road racing on a shoestring almost from the beginning. One of the best known Bantam tuning outfits who also used to sell road bike spares, Bernie's Spares and Repairs of Watford, in the end used to send out a Q. and A. sheet with their pricelists to pre-empt some inevitable questions such as:

Q. What can I do to make my Bantam go faster? I can only spend £22 on it.

A. Nothing, apart from ride it down a steep hill.

They went on to spell out that if you were prepared to spend a lot of money (often on parts from the later D14/4 and B175 models, which are the ones we will be mainly interested in anyway) 'You may see the upper eighties out of it, but it will be difficult to ride in traffic and subject to constant maintenance if it's to remain reliable.' We second this voice of experience, and are looking for a long and trouble-free life, not a screamer.

The same thing by and large goes for the Villiers singles and twins. There were several square-barrelled performance kits for the 197cc 9E and later the A series, from Vale Onslow of Birmingham, Parkinson, Marcelle and the bike makers Greeves and DMW, who were at the forefront of those squeezing more power out of the Villiers single-cylinder engine (the Hogans

Above: ***Sorry, not our patch.*** *A Greeves Silverstone sprinter rearranges eardrums at a Barbon hillclimb.*

Left: *A square-barrelled Villiers-engined James scrambler in action, too fast and fragile for our purposes.*

did the same for Bantams). The kits usually offered an alloy barrel which, following Greeves' lead, would be square-finned, and enlarged the dimensions to 250 with a piston, head and long studs to suit. But Villiers bottom ends were often not equal to the power increase; cranks would spread where the pin and webs were machined into the crankshaft, causing crank flexing which worked the mains loose. Likewise with the twin; the basic 249cc 2T, with 8.2:1 compression ratio, was bored out to become the 324cc 3T in 1958, but the latter, at first intended for use in light cars and three wheelers, had a lower 7.25:1 compression and soon, lower gearing. Harshness and a drop in reliability only appeared with the 1964-on 249cc engine, the 17bhp 4T. Any attempt to go beyond the 3T is inadvisable, and not only because of the cycle parts in which most of the twins are mounted. Twin enthusiast Dave Benson got Villiers' expert Alf Snell to build him a bored-out 3T with barrels off 197cc singles, but the result was only 2hp up on the 3T's 16.5 at 5000rpm, and fuel consumption rose very dramatically. Just comparing these power outputs with today's sports 125s reveals the futility of tweaking the old dears. 2T-engined machines in stock form can make a pleasant and lively enough mount with a satisfying harmony between engine and bicycle, and that's what it's all about.

In the same way that this book will not be orientated towards concours restoration of the selected models, it will also not provide the details necessary for stripdowns, or even basic workshop techniques. Though again it will provide details of where such information can be found, our intention ('Practical' once more) is to get the bikes going and suitable for regular use, which as indicated does not include so highly polished that you come to dread a rain shower. As many practical tips to that end will be included as possible.

Lastly, as you will have gathered, this book does not attempt to cover every British lightweight. It is intended that four-strokes will be dealt with in a later companion volume, and in any case they tend to be slightly pricier propositions. Of the two-strokes, there is no consideration of the Royal Enfield 125 Ensign or Prince, which are both too slow and too rare (and today, quite sought after in British two-stroke circles). None of Excelsior's own-brand twin cylinder engined machines are dealt with for the same consideration of rarity. British Anzani twin cylinder engines powered early machines from Greeves, Norman, etc., but as they were neither lively nor particularly reliable, and as engine spares today are very difficult, they fall outside the 'Practical' parameters.

On the positive side, I shall go over the models in question to show why particular types and years are recommended. For those that know the scene, there will be few revelations, but rehearsing the history may help you to resist the temptation to succumb to a particularly attractive example of a bike which could turn into a money-trap, or not meet the 'Practical' requirements.

Chapter 4

Where have they all gone? - and the numbers game

A preliminary question is why, if so many of these lightweights were produced, are so few apparently still with us, compared to the high-profile big British four-strokes? One part of the answer also directly concerns money, so this seems the place to deal with it.

The main reason for comparative scarcity is something once described as 'The more there were, the less there are' syndrome. As utility machines, the lightweights were used hard, and often thoroughly abused by novice riders and mechanics, and being numerous and not perceived as valuable, they were then discarded when worn out.

Since then, the ones that have remained in Britain have been further diminished by two further factors. The first is export. Since interest in 'classic' machinery began to rise in the mid-70s, the export of old British machines to Europe, Australia and Japan has steadily increased, but being an expensive process, naturally it has tended to centre on the more desirable large four-stroke models. However, an exception arose when Japan's *shaken*, their version of the MOT which takes up most of a day, became so fierce in its standards for lights, brakes, etc., that it effectively excluded a big 'classic' from road use in that country. The *shaken*, however, only applied to machines over 250cc, and the result was an outflow of smaller British machines for high prices, though these tended to be shiny models like the Tiger Cub and C15. Well, everyone gets what they deserve.

More complicated and potentially more serious is the peculiarly British situation over the sale of old-style registration numbers. From 1904 when the first index marks were allocated, until 1963, a registration mark initially consisted of letters first and then numbers — either two letters and four numbers, two letters and three numbers, or three letters and three numbers. In the late 50s and early 60s when three letter and three number combinations began to be used up, they were reversed, so that the numbers came first and the letters second. Then from February 1963, registration marks carried a letter after them, or suffix, beginning with A and working

Owned by the BSA Group in the 60s, and seen here on a Triumph TR25W Trophy, a badge-engineered version of BSA's B25 250 single. What would this registration be worth to some pop mogul today?

through the alphabet, which clearly indicated the 12-month period during which the registration was issued. For some time this applied to England and Wales only, as Scotland's supply of number and letter registrations was far from exhausted.

Pre-suffix numbers thus have become desirable, for two reasons. They appeal to the vanity market with the names they spell, or the initials they form (SUE, JON, HRH, etc.) and with the vehicles to which they allude — 450 SL for a Mercedes, for instance, or simply the letters 911, 924, 928, etc., for a Porsche. The BSA group at one time held BSA 1, which it shuttled between test bikes and a black cab built by another group subsidiary, Carbodies.

The other and more substantial use is as 'cover' numbers to conceal the age of coaches and limousines belonging to hire companies, and of the luxury vehicles of private owners. Both parties wish their vehicles to seem either timeless, or newer than they actually are. Either way, the pre-suffix numbers have become sought after, and the situation intensified after November 1983, when the licensing authority, which since the early 70s had been the DVLC at Swansea, 'closed the record'. This meant that if you had an old vehicle off the road, with an old-style buff or green fold-out logbook issued by the former local Licensing Authority, unless you had heard about the recall and got your vehicle and its number registered on an equivalent V5 registration document from Swansea, the old number was lost. This can present you with a minor problem if the lightweight you buy falls into this category and has to be re-registered. The necessary procedure when doing so will be found described on p135. Numbers dealers believe that up to half the old-style registrations disappeared when the records were closed, and the price of what was left has risen accordingly.

What this has meant is that even an indistinguished pre-suffix number is now saleable. What it also means is a potential dilemma for anyone buying a pre-'63 British lightweight with an original number, because while some see selling the registration as a legitimate way for the less well off to help pay for their motorcycling, others view it as repugnant behaviour which separates a bike from its history (and, in the case of a desirable machine, lowers its value). For first, the two, or the last two of the three letter parts of the registrations were not allocated at random, but indicated the area or the licensing authority where they were issued. My own first Volkswagen Beetle, registered in Norwich, had a memorable and characteristic BAH! The regional letter coding used to be listed at the front of old AA books, and today can be found, together with long alphabetical lists which in many cases also indicate the month and year of issue, in a booklet called *Where's It From and When Was It Issued?* (for details of which, see the end of this section).

Secondly, motorcycle dealers kept records of the registration numbers allocated to the new machines they sold, and many of these are now held by London's Science Museum Library, in Exhibition Road, South Kensington, London SW7 2DD (Tel: 01-581-4734). You can contact them and arrange to look at the relevant records, and if your machine proves to be among these records, you can discover its place of origin and the original owner. If the old-style, fold-out logbook, with its useful record of every owner, has been either lost or handed in to Swansea, this can be the only chance you have to be able to find out any of your individual machine's history.

Many of the lightweights this book considers were made after the 1963 cut-off point, so for them none of this is relevant. Perhaps, too, such considerations do not concern you much, but for people with an interest in old machines, the opposite may very well be the case, and they tend to frown on the sale of numbers. So if you do come into possession of a pre-suffix number and decide to sell it on, it would be inadvisable to 18 broadcast the fact at your local VMCC section! There are legitimate occasions for selling, such as when a machine is to go for export abroad (another practice of which some disapprove), or to be converted solely for competition use; and some argue that for utility machines, being less intrinsically interesting (and valuable) the arguments against the practice are weakened. With the closing of the records in 1983, it is now much less likely that an owner would have taken the trouble to preserve a number and yet be unaware of its potential value, particularly since both the motorcycle and local press often carry the small ads. of dealers offering to buy anything on two wheels pre-1963. (This, of course, has put up the price of lightweights, especially at auctions, and also diminishes the pool of them, as some will be discarded once the number has been sold, though most are passed on to dealers, once again meaning higher prices.) The world is full of strange circumstances, however, and if in a Welsh barnyard you should discover a Francis-Barnett Fulmar with a V5 bearing the mark POR 911, and you buy it, you could have acquired something worth in excess of £15,000.

I should hasten to add that ordinary numbers are worth a great deal less than that, on average for a three letter/three number registration perhaps £350-£400; of this you will see between £200 and £300 if you sell, as most do, via a numbers agent, and his fee has been deducted. If you sell direct to the dealer, for an immediate result, the sum will be reduced still further. Some numbers are said to be virtually unnegotiable, such as those three letter/three figure ones with V, X, Y in the letters as these are unlikely to be in anybody's initials, but if the letters are followed by two numbers, they become desirable again. The decision to sell or not is entirely your own, but if you do decide to do so and make your lightweight project partly self-financing, here is how to go about it.

1.   The machine has to have a V5, and the frame number on the machine has to be the same as the one recorded on the V5; variations of perhaps one or two numbers may be permitted as inaccurate transcription onto the original documents is not unknown, but it has to be very close. And the machine has to be roadworthy and hold an MOT, or have held one a few weeks previously.

2.   Find a numbers dealer from the ones who advertise in *Exchange and Mart* or the *Sunday Times*. It is advisable that they should be members of the trade organisation, the CNDA (Cherished Numbers Dealers Association) to keep you clear of real cowboys. Offer the number to two or three, to get an idea of prices, but not too many, as if you have a desirable number, competition between them to get you on their list may lead you to being quoted an unrealistically high price, which you will never in fact see. That is if you choose to let the numbers dealer act as your agent, and sell on your behalf for an agreed commission. If you sell to the dealer direct, it will be immediate, but for less.

3.   Now you wait while the dealer advertises your number. The average waiting time is around six months, though sales pick up over the 19

Christmas period (yuppie presents). It can be up to a year. You can check the dealers' adverts to see what he is offering the number for. Many people will let the dealer hold the logbook during this period, though the cautious will prefer to retain it themselves.

4.   When a buyer appears, the dealer will contact you and ask you to arrange a date for the machine to be inspected at the Local Vehicle Licensing Office (LVLO) nearest to where you, as the vendor, live. If the dealer is holding both the documents, once you have fixed the date and let him know, he will post them to the LVLO. If you are holding your document, the dealer will send you the buyer's document and you take both to the LVLO with your machine on the appointed day, plus the MOT certificate for your machine. Usually one up to six months out of date is also OK, but check with the LVLO; and your machine should be generally roadworthy.

5.   The inspection at the LVLO is essentially to check that your frame number is the same as that on your V5 document, and it does not normally involve more than that. If the LVLO are satisfied, the sale will go through (costing the buyer of your number a £70 fee) and you will be issued with a new number, almost always one with an A-suffix. This will be issued to you within two weeks of the inspection, and sometimes sooner. ('Q' numbers are issued under other circumstances, such as when a machine is imported from abroad, or when a frame, which for registration purposes represents the vehicle, is fitted with an engine other than the one on the original document relating to it. 'Q' numbers are definitely a bit declassé in British motorcycling circles, and will lower a machine's value). You should be paid the agreed sum by your numbers agent within two weeks. If not, contact the CNDA; your local Citizens Advice Bureau or Trading Standards Department may also be able to help.

Note, however, that a low value number cannot be regarded as a good reason for adding that value to the sale price of a machine. Many fall into this trap and over-price their machines, seriously reducing their sales prospects.

Stop Press: *Just as this book was on its way to the printers (October 1989), news came of a probable change of heart on the part of the DVLC. It seems that in the face of continuous presure from the VMCC, the RAC and many other old vehicle groups, before long an owner will be able to register with Swansea an old machine which lacks a V5, and retains its original registration number. It is said that these numbers will not be transferable (i.e. you won't be able to sell them to a numbers dealer) and neither in future will age-related numbers. So check with the VMCC or the BMF before proceeding on any of the above advice.*

That is enough about number sales, not a particularly elevating topic but an inevitable part of the British bike scene at present. Now to consider the more cheerful prospect of looking for an actual lightweight motorcycle.

Chapter Five

Have you got room? - and the B and C factor

Before the search begins in earnest, there are some things to check first. Accumulating the necessary cash to do it right is the first. Next there's the matter of whether you have the time and the temperament to take on something which will involve some work, some chasing around after parts, and some regular maintenance. Only you can answer that one. After that, if you do find what you've decided to look for, have you got anywhere to keep it?

This sounds like an obvious one. If you have a garage that is not completely full of car, no problem. If you have access to a family garage, perhaps you can bargain temporary space in it for necessary work, keeping the bike on the street for the rest of the time. If you have a house or a flat with a garden that a bike can be pushed through to, or even a front garden area, again no problem. But for many, the machine will have to reside on the streets, where it will be vulnerable to weather and to thieves.

The first protection against either is a cover, and the importance of using one cannot be overstressed. Without it, even if the machine is in poor condition already, it will certainly get worse, as while dirt attacks the paint and chrome, rain gets into the cables, electrics and the seat — not nice. The likelihood of theft or vandalism on an uncovered machine also greatly increases — out of sight, out of the tiny minds of the yahoos seems to be the case. The cover ideally should be of the green treated canvas kind, or a tarpaulin, both of which 'breathe', whereas plastic such as PVC traps moisture within it. But a plastic groundsheet may do as a temporary cover, and certainly is the only thing that will fold up small enough to take with you on your touring travels, where an overnight cover for the controls, electrics and seat is no less vital than at home. However, a new green canvas cover costs over £20 and may even be the object of theft itself! Some people paint their machine registration number on the cover to deter this. A used one, or a large piece of tarpaulin may be preferable, though handling it may provide the first of several contacts with the dirt which using British motorcycles seems inevitably to bring with it.

The next thing is a lock of some kind, and it should be remembered that this will have to be carried about with you on journeys, to secure the bike at the far end. The best locks are the shackle kind shaped like an elongated D, such as the *Kryptonite* range. They are quite portable, but they cost at least £22, and they cannot secure a machine by its frame to a permanent, immovable object like a lamp post. A good length of thick chain covered in plastic, and a large brass-bodied padlock can do that, but they will be heavy to carry — flamboyant riders can wear them round the waist or slung like a bandolier across the shoulders, but road dirt will distribute itself about your clothes and person once again if you do this! Still, at around £10, especially if you can find an ironmonger or wholesalers to cut the chain to length, this is probably the best compromise.

Not many of the utility machines carry built-in steering-head locks; the Bantam was an exception, fitting one from 1956 to 1959, after which it was replaced by a hole in a special frame lug, which when you turn the fork to the left lines up with a corresponding hole in the bottom yoke lug. Slip a padlock through both to lock them together, and the bike is temporarily secure. I say temporarily because either picking the padlock or a few minutes' work with a hacksaw will overcome it. To the determined professional, the same is true of most locks, and unless chained to something immovable, motorcycles can always be lifted into a van and driven away to be worked on at leisure. But the comparatively low value of these utility bikes means that they should not be at risk from professionals, just joyriders and vandals, and this partial immunity is a big practical plus point for the

Sadly, a beautifully restored lightweight like this GPO Bantam could be a prime target for thieves. Cover it up and lock it.

lightweights. If your machine is particualrly cherished, and lives outside your window, there's an Oxford Fairings mini-alarm which you might care to consider at just under £20.

Where do you find a used piece of tarpaulin or a good secondhand padlock? One answer is to invoke the B and C factor. That's Biddies and Codgers, the senior citizens of your acquaintance, whether neighbours, relatives or people you meet at work, the shops or the pub. Once you're interested in old motorbikes and let this fact be known to them, the pensioner can cease to be a b.o.f. and become the source of clean cotton rags (the only kind for polishing), clear plastic bags (more of which later), old tools, oil cans, padlocks, tarpaulin and maybe even a shed to work in and an extra pair of experienced hands to help. With the right Codger a Francis-Barnett can leap the generation gap faster than Evel Knievel clearing the Grand Canyon. Older people can also be a great source of information, not just word of mouth and local knowledge (someone used to have one of those and bits might still be around, etc.) but outside London they also often read the local paper with the same minute attention which a Witness gives his Bible, and once they've locked on to the fact that you are interested, will relay every bit of information on local events and on machines for sale.

This brings us to the question of where you search for your machine. Newsagents' boards used to be good, but are not much use for older machines any more. Local papers are not frequent enough sources to be worth buying specially, but if they're in your household anyway, start scanning the For Sale ads, or make sure your B and C irregulars are doing it for you. **Exchange and Mart** used to be good, but is now only worth a glance in the newsagents. The most obvious sources, **Classic Bike** and **The Classic Motor Cycle** magazines are not necessarily the best, if only because advertising in them is comparatively expensive, and so will attract those with the more expensive models to dispose of; but cheaper machinery and bargains can feature, particularly in the cheaper 'Autojumble' readers' ads section in **Classic Bike.** However, it's always worth reading all the ads carefully, as a Bantam or other lightweight may be tacked onto the details of a larger bike for sale, or feature as part of a 'garage clearance'. The same thing goes for the weekly paper, **Motor Cycle News** — it's worth reading the small ads with care as lightweights, particularly Bantams, can crop up in the general 'Machines for Sale' section as well as in the tailor-made post-vintage advertisement column.

However, the place to look for cheap bikes is cheap adverts, or better still, free ones. At the time of writing (1989) **Classic Mechanics** has a free readers' ads section, as does the likeable **Classic Motorcycle Legends. British Bike Magazine** has some readers' free ads, and the bizarrely named **Silver Machine** features the same free ads as its predecessor **Motor Cycle Enthusiast.** One of the best is the irreverent handbook-sized **Used Motorcycle Guide (UMG)** at just 99p a copy, with 16 pages of Free Ads — don't confuse **UMG** with its similar format imitator **Used and Classic Bike Guide,** which also features free ads but rather less of them, as yet. At £23.75 a year, **Old Bike Mart** is also an excellent source.

Good condition, but expect to pay dealers' prices. A pre-1953 plunger D1 fronts a line of Bantams outside a shop. Registration number's A-suffix indicates that the original number has been sold on already.

In all these cases it is taken for granted that you will be scanning the private ads and not the dealers' ones, either those that cater exclusively for classic machinery or the modern shops that do a side-line in old bikes. Prices there are inevitably a third to a half as much again as in a private sale, and if a bike is offered cheaply or 'as seen', it's more than likely that it will need work doing to it which will make up or exceed the price differential. You may be able to trade in your old Japanese machinery at a dealer, and the better ones may offer some sort of guarantee on what you buy, but at our level of budget, private is almost certainly best. In order to make sure that an advertised bike is a genuine private sale rather than a dealer working out of his home, when you ring up simply say 'I've called about the bike', and if the reply is 'Which one?', counter with 'Which ones have you got?'. If the list is substantial, you have probably struck the Trade again rather than your ideal, a privately owned bike whose keeper has owned, used, and looked after it for a fair length of time. Auctions and autojumbles (as a source for worthwhile complete lightweight machines) can also usually be discounted, though there are exceptions.

Naturally, purchasing all the magazines mentioned above will stretch the budget unnecessarily. **UMG** and **MCN** might be bought, though if you live in town the latter weekly is stocked by most public lending and reference libraries. If you live in London, incidentally, MCN can sometimes be found on sale in some central newsagents (try around Tottenham Court Road) the day before the Wednesday on which it is due to come out, which gives you a little head start. For the others, and for magazines which themselves may yield what you desire, it's time to consider the Club.

Chapter Six
In the club

Why should you join a motorcycle club before you have a motorcycle? The answer is that membership of some of them is a prerequisite to an excellent and economic insurance scheme, and it also makes sense in a number of other ways that help you select a machine sensibly and save money once you have done so. If your spirit sinks at the very notion of clubability, or you live in a remote area of the country where getting to club branch meetings is not a possibility (or if you just don't feel inclined to attend them), you should still think about joining.

Membership probably gives you the insurance scheme. It gives you a free club magazine, which has ads for spares and for bikes, very possibly the ones you're looking for, at prices generally somewhat restrained by the knowledge that fellow club members will be seeing them, and often by a genuine wish that a machine 'goes to a good home'. It has experts on each model and sometimes sub-sections thereof (there are early and late Bantam specialists in the BSA Owners Club, for instance) to whom you can write with queries. It usually has a library which for a nominal fee will provide copies of articles, road tests and other literature which will help you build up valuable knowledge of your intended mount and influence your choice. In some cases it will offer a Spares Scheme, and also the hire of specialist tools, as well as services sometimes unobtainable anywhere else. Finally, once you have your machine, membership often will entitle you to discounts of 10% and sometimes 15% at selected shops and dealers specialising in your marque.

If you do live within reach of a branch and can get to meetings even occasionally, the situation improves dramatically. Other members can let you know the good and the bad points of local suppliers, bike shops and services — and sometimes even the particular old bikes for sale in an area! They can often lend you current literature, both books and magazines — as I said, if you tot up the roll call of periodicals in which to check the

Above: **Happy 60th Birthday, lightweights.** The British Two-Stroke Club celebrates its Diamond Jubilee with a lavish display at the 1989 Bristol Classic Show.

Below: *The Bantam Owners Club fields an impressive line-up at the start of their 1988 Cockerel Run. The guy on the far end appears to be a sore loser.*

ads listed in the previous section, at around £1.50 each, the total monthly expenditure is just too much, though it is worth buying, say, one copy of *Classic Bike* for the shop and service ads, preferably the one, usually in October, where they include a 'Parts and Services Guide' supplement with many useful addresses. Your fellow club members will probably have back numbers with articles on your range of machines, and the relevant marque histories and restoration guides. These can also be sought at your local library, but not every library can provide books which are not already on its shelves. More of that in Section III.

The club people will also help focus your mind on your choice of machine. Printed sources and your own imaginings are all very well, but there is no substitute for talking to people who have acutally owned and run a particular machine for some time. They will not only convey the warts-and-all picture, but will help you square it up with your requirements. Will it be fast enough to satisfy? Will it carry a passenger adequately if you need to do so regularly? Will it be up to the journeys you will want to make, whether for commuting, camping weekends, or touring further afield? Reliable enough? Without any fatal spares gaps? A satisfying machine for you to own? With luck, if you have a licence you may even get a ride on an example of the machine you are interested in, or at the least, if you have a helmet, a ride on the pillion.

Perhaps most valuable of all, a club member would probably be willing to go along with you and check out machines which you are interested in buying. Even if you are an experienced motorcyclist with a good knowledge of your model, this is invaluable, because your companion, although he may be keen on the model himself, will be at least a little more disinterested than you are, as someone gripped with the lust to pay whatever's asked, snap up an example of your cult object, and get on with riding it. Two heads **are** better than one - between you, you are more likely to remember to ask all the things that need to be asked. Tactically and psychologically, it's better too — you will feel less uncertain, and can withdraw into a huddle together and shake your heads before emerging with a somewhat reduced offer.

Further than that, if you buy the bike, a club member will very possibly be able to help you get it back to where you live, since the ideal combination of a machine that is running, taxed and has an MOT does not come up very often, and your insurance may not yet be arranged. The club may have the use of a van, or a car with a towing bracket and trailer; or if a van has to be hired, they should know the cheapest place locally, and may be able to split the cost by using it for other members' business as well. Further alternatives in this line are to use your own or your family's hatchback or estate car, probably after first removing one or both of the bike's wheels. Even with plenty of plastic sheeting and old blankets to absorb spillage, this arrangement is not ideal. I have had a 650 twin in the back of an Astra, but it didn't do the car's rear sill any good, and though lightweights are less of a strain, the danger of disfiguring the tin box is not negligible. Another possibility, if you know that you will **27**

British two-stroke ownership could always include trips abroad, as the Clubs well know. Here 'Flasher' Rogers sets out from the Ariel Works in Birmingham for the Monte Carlo rally on his fully-equipped Ariel Leader.

be having engine or other work done by a local British bike shop or specialist, is to arrange for their van to collect the machine.

The clubs organize runs and rallies, and they may also be involved in pre-'65 off-road sport, in which there is a resurgence of interest at present. Pukka trials and scrambles versions of the lightweights, like their heavyweight four-stroke brothers, will be higher-priced than the equivalent road-going machines, either Bantams or Villiers 9E-engined or similar machinery. Don Morley's three books for Osprey on Classic British Off-road bikes can tell you what's what in this field, and your club can be a way to involvement — but space does not allow this book to concern itself with anything but roadsters.

Finally, either the club or individual members may be able to let you use a garage or workshop for necessary tasks, or while your machine is laid up. All in all, clubs are a Good Thing. As well as the practical advantages from your side, you may find that you have something to contribute, and you may make some friends.

With most of the models, you will be eligible for membership of more than one club. With a Bantam, for instance, there's the VMCC for a machine more than 25 years old, the BSA Owners Club, the Bantam Owners Club and the British Two-Stroke Club. If more than one meets in your area, it may be worthwhile getting the details via a contact address from the BMF (whose own permanent address will be found at the end of this section),

Local all-British bike clubs welcome lightweights, as evidenced by this nicely restored 1966 D7 de Luxe Bantam under the BBA banner.

and going along to see which of them is most congenial - club branches do sometimes orient along age lines, and have distinctive characters.

The VMCC, the vintage Motor Cycle Club, is the big nationwide one, with more than 8000 members where few others manage 2000. If 'Vintage' conjures gents in deerstalkers and plus-fours on pre-war machinery, this is not at all the case, as they are men and women of all ages, lively and humorous as well as often deeply informed, and they ride anything up to 25 years old in addition to modern machinery, often enough. The subscription is the highest, at £18 currently, but the range of services on offer is the greatest, including marque specialists with expert free advice and the insurance scheme, which they organise.

Relevant clubs are listed at the end of the appropriate sections, together with whether or not they are eligible for the insurance scheme. If the contact addresses given should have become out of date, contact the BMF for a full club directory with an up-to-date address. The directory will also include another option, local clubs for British bikes. You will also often find details of these at your nearest British bike shop. If there is one in your area, they are very often more lively socially than the one-make clubs.

Chapter Seven

Horse-trading, or fowl practices

It should first be said that the best money-saving device when buying a secondhand bike is time. If you allow yourself the time, and are patient enough, sooner or later a bargain will present itself. While fantastic bargains are rare and should not be counted on, a low initial purchase price — for a machine in reasonable order, of course — is the single biggest factor in keeping the overall cost of the project down.

So — you've become enthused over and educated about a particular model, chewed it over with club people, got the money together and made the other necessary arrangements. You find a likely small ad and ring up. (If you do even a fair bit of ringing around, there's an invaluable publication detailing the geographical location of dialling prefixes, so that if a number's area is beyond your reach of travel, you needn't waste a call. Details at the end of this section.) The bike is still available; as far as you can, check on the phone that it is what you actually think that it is, and hopefully has a V5 document. You contact your co-conspirator in the club or a knowledgeable friend or relative, and go for it.

A few ground rules. Take the means of payment, preferably in cash — waving actual currency, corny as it is, does sometimes get the price down, and if it's a cheque, or even a banker's draft in todays' naughty world, you probably won't be able to take the machine home then and there, which you want to do if possible. Take your helmet and riding gear — you may be allowed a test ride (very desirable) if you leave your friend and transport as security, or at least the owner may take you on the pillion. If at all possible, go in daylight, though if it is midweek in winter, this may not be possible.

There is a lot of detailed advice on checking used motorcycles and your 'rabbi' should know most of it — testing for play in the forks, steering head and wheel bearings, checking the suspension, state of the tyres, rear chain and battery, etc. Since you're after a runner, the machine should start, the electrical equipment work, it should move off and not sound too rough.

Would you buy a used lightweight from this man? The author in Fat Man of Highbury mode, gets a buyer from the younger generation hooked on Bantam power in the shape of his late B175.

Ask to see the V5 and check the details, registration, engine and especially frame number against the actual machine. Note the number plates and compare it with the V5, irrespective of whether you intend selling the number or not, as an original number naturally affects the value of the machine when you come to sell it in your turn. If it's a 50s or 60s machine with a 'first registered date' on the V5 after 1983, and probably an S in the second of the last two registration letters, the original number is likely to have gone and it bears an age-related one. If it's an A-suffix number for anything other than a machine first registered in 1963, the original number has probably been sold.

Anything worn or defective which will need renewing — especially tyres at £25 or more a throw — should be bartered against the asking price, as should major deviations from standard condition which you will know about from your swotting up on the model (whether or not they are in fact important to you, once again they affect the resale value). The same things goes for the absence of an MOT and/or road tax. Extra equipment and spares etc., offered should not be allowed to raise a price significantly.

There is a fine line between legitimate haggling and 'time-wasting', i.e. offering an unrealistically low price. You should have a fair idea of average prices from your scanning of the small ads; some people even tot up all the prices and divide them by the number of machines, but this does not really allow for the fact than an asking price will not necessarily be paid, or for nuances of condition and the overall feel of the proposition. This includes the seller. They come in all shapes and sizes, but ideally should be an older person who has had the bike for some time, used it regularly but not excessively, and cared for it, which will be evident from both the overall condition, the things that the seller knows and says, and the absence of chewed up screws and bolt heads. The ideal seldom materialises.

All being well, your adviser in agreement, you take the plunge, pay, put your transport arrangements into operation, and the beast is yours. That's when you begin to find out what it's really like!

Useful information

Publications
COLLECTING, RESTORING AND RIDING CLASSIC MOTORCYCLES by Tim Holmes and Rebekka Smith (Patrick Stephens Ltd, price £6.99): a general guide with good background information.

WHERE'S IT FROM AND WHEN WAS IT ISSUED? (Transport Bookman Publications Ltd., Syon Park, Brentford, London TW8 8SF, price £2.95)

TELEPHONE DIALLING CODE LOCATION GUIDE, PMS, Market Square. Chambers, Market Square, Congleton CW12 1ET.

Clubs
The Vintage Motor Cycle Club Ltd. (VMCC), 138 Derby Street, Burton on Trent, Staffordshire DE14 2LF. Tel: (0283) 40557.

British Motorcyclists Federation (BMF), Jack Wiley House, 129 Seaforth Avenue, Motspur Park, New Malden, Surrey. Tel: 01-942 7914.

Chapter Eight

The BSA Bantam

Bantam Background

With British lightweights, first, last and always, it's the BSA Bantam. Indeed, in Britain in the 50s and early 60s the word 'Bantam' became as synonymous with any kind of light bike as 'Hoover' did with all vacuum cleaners. Records are incomplete, but it seems that between 350,000 and half a million of the little two-stroke single cylinder machines were produced, between late 1948 and the end, early in 1971. As '50s publicity put it, 'You can't beat a Bantam'.

The D1 Bantam engine was fundamentally a German DKW design taken by the Allies as war reparation. Today's MZ125 is a direct descendant of the original design, but BSA swapped metric measurements to inches and redesigned the engine in a 'mirror image' to put the gearchange on the right, in line with British practice. This also put the primary drive on the right, which was unusual for a British machine. From then on, Bantam development kept strict pace with the DKW; the latter's successful RT175, having a 174cc engine of 62 x 58mm dimensions, was followed by the Bantam 175 D5, not very different at 61.5 x 58mm/172cc.

Bantams were built at BSA's Redditch factory at a rate of 400 a week in their 50s heyday. With their 48lb engine weight and the D1's low 153lb overall dry weight, plus the low saddle height, they were an instant hit with non-enthusiast riders of both sexes. Their full size wheels gave them the edge over their market rivals, continental scooters, on the unmade roads that covered much of the world and particularly the Commonwealth, a big BSA market in the 50s. Peggy Iris Thomas, with her Airedale terrier on the pillion, exemplified the bold touring a Bantam could allow, and her book on a trans-American journey, *A Ride in the Sun*, was a big success. Though BSA were committed to heavyweights for off-road sports, a trials D1 was marketed. Later, the Bushman, an off-road variant purpose-built for Australia and elsewhere, provided the basis of a works trials machine that in 1967 was placed 2nd in the Scottish Six Days Trial. Even more impressive in its way was how the familiar red-painted Post Office Bantams survived up

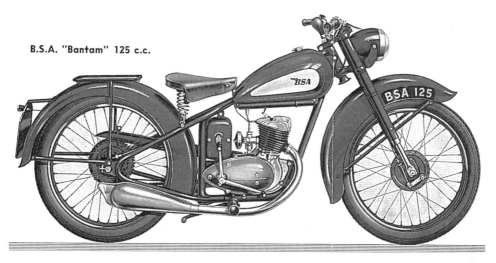

B.S.A. "Bantam" 125 c.c.

Above: *D1 Bantam for 1948/9.*

Below: *Highly recommended. One of the author's Bantams, a 1970 B175 complete with obligatory non-functioning centre-stand plus proprietary pressed-steel luggage rack.*

to six year's service apiece in the hands of 16 to 18 year old telegram delivery boys.

Riding a Bantam today exposes you to a torrent of usually affectionate reminiscence from a great multitude of older people. Like Oscar Wilde who remarked while he was on trial that 'London is behind me — to a boy', both boys and girls of all ages are frequently galvanised and enthused by the sight of what was so often their first transport. Notwithstanding a lack of development and a few flaws, Bantams were genuinely likeable machines, cheap, tough, light and undemanding — and also, which should not be ignored, they were good-looking. 'Pretty' is the word that usually comes to mind, especially for the all-Mist Green early D1 with sprung saddle and bulb horn fixed on the fork crown, with cream yellow, gold-lined tank panels decorated with the proud cockerel transfer. The middle period, with early 175 D7s echoing the BSA C15 series four-stroke singles with headlamp nacelle, and side and centre panel covers, plus larger petrol tanks in primary red or blue colours, some of the later ones even with chrome side panels and pear-shaped plastic badges, may seem a bit stodgy. The later, more angular models with their gaitered forks and chromed kidney-shaped tanks, can be very striking - the polychromatic red, extra chromed D10 and D14/4 Sports models were particularly spiffy, and if a Tiger Cub was known as a Baby Bonnie, a black and chrome B175 could surely qualify as a Tiny Thunderbolt.

I must declare an interest, having owned several (a clutch of Bantams?), worked despatch riding on one in London in the 70s, written them into a thriller (*Dealer's Wheels*), and ridden another to Crete and back. Running one alongside more powerful machinery, it was so often a relief to step back for town work onto the Bantam, which would get you there every time, and when you got there, was light enough to haul up on to pavements and park propped against walls (that centre stand!). Yet the same bike would carry a fair load of luggage and put in just about 200 touring miles in a day, too — on the return leg of the Crete trip, across Italy from Venice to Genoa, was one such day, and a brief account of a Bantam touring jaunt in England will be found at the end of this volume. The Bantam was similar to a VW Beetle (I owned several of those as well, an equally damaging admission to a speed merchant). Both provided indifferent but acceptable roadholding and handling, and unexciting but utterly reliable power, while somehow contriving to be obscurely satisfying to ride and drive.

Except for my first Bantam, a swinging-arm 175cc D7, which was virtually a Norfolk field bike, and for another three-speed D7 which I bought to sell, all the operational machines I owned were of the last B175 variety, and these are the ones which seemed to me above all to qualify for the 'Practical' tag. Yet one conventional view is that the soft, low-powered early rigid or plunger D1s were the best of the lot. Certainly, the 4.5bhp 125s and their today rather rare 150cc D3 Major derivatives, have great charm and can provide a pleasant potter round the lanes and along country tracks.

But they are underpowered for today's roads, somewhat under-braked, and none of their electrical systems (which came in battery or direct lighting form) can be relied upon to provide ignition *and* lights consistently, which is obviously another practical requirement.

From 1958 came the early 7.4bhp 175s, in D7 Super form from 1959, and once again in the opinion of some, these were the best compromise. The late Bob Currie, a motorcycle journalist so enamoured of the products of Birmingham that once when he was working in London he would travel miles to buy household goods manufactured and packaged in Brum, considered that the '61 D7 Super de Luxe "Represented the little BSA at very nearly its best". Pointing out that an understressed engine tends towards reliability and longevity, he thought that later models, while enjoying a 4-speed gearbox, were 'a bit revvy and peaky'. (It was true that the 1967-on alternator models had less flywheel effect.)

Others see it differently, however. British 2-stroke expert Nick Kelly having owned an early D7, though admittedly a Villiers fan, considers that they were 'Nasty — they cheapened everything. On the flywheel mag models they increased the width of the Woodruff key without increasing the width of the crankshaft, which sometimes snapped'. And it was partly the early 175's 3-speed box that told against them, and not just because of the large jumps between the widely-spaced gears which had always characterised it. Especially in its pre-'67 form, when the power increase had not been matched by a strengthened design — and even that was often stressed by the 1967 D10's 40% output increase. There were potential problems with the 175's 3-speed box, detailed later, which led to jumping out of gear, particularly 2nd, when in worn condition, which a 30-year-old example is most likely to be. The Bantam's unit construction, disliked by some as evidence of Teutonic efficiency-mindedness, which was all very well until things went wrong, makes the gearbox less than an easy job to work on. Bike-writing rebel Royce Creasey, writing from punishing experience with a 3-speed D10, snarled that 'The gearbox must stand as the most inadequate system for providing a variable-step power transmission yet invented'. This is hyperbole, or all the epic journeys achieved by 3-speed D1s (see the accompanying publicity poster on p10/11 for a selection of them) would never have been achieved. But the 175's 3-speed till 1967 did represent a step backward, and for old Bantams; Creasey is probably right when he judges that the gearbox and electrics make up 75% of their problems.

If the D1-D5 represented the Bantam's youth, and the D7 its middle years, the final '67-'71 175s, the D10-B175, in the eyes of some were not so much maturity as a flaming menopause. The '67 D10 which came in four varieties, two 3-speed, two 4-speed, and all with improved electrics, reached speeds in the mid-60s, and the following year power was increased by a further 3 horses to nearly 13bhp — the first 700 or so 1968 machines went out as 'D13s', but after that superstition prevailed and they bore D14/4 tag, the latter part indicating that all models were now 4-speed. So were the '68 machines the ultimates? No, because the power step had been achieved in part by discs on the flywheels which were now attached by **37**

Nearly the best, or cheapened? A trio of likely lads take delivery of a pair fo new D7 Bantam 175 Super models. Were they in for unpleasant surprises?

rivets, which at high speed (and through vibration) not infrequently worked loss and trashed the engine. Small end failures and crankpin breakages were also not unkown.

These problems were dealt with for the final model, which came into production from February 1969 and engine No. BC00115. Its nomenclature is slightly disputed; the BSA two-strokes had always carried a 'D' prefix, but by that time there were men in charge of the company who had scant respect for tradition. Though some of the technical literature continued to call this model the 'D175', or even at first during 1969, the 'D14/4' still, elsewhere from 1970 it was referred to as simply the Bantam 175, or (spuriously claiming the prefix from their current range of four-stroke singles), the B175. In the interests of clarity, B175 is how the model will be referred to in this book; this extended explanation is given because a late Bantam may be advertised as any of these things, and the B175s really were stronger, as will be detailed below, and while undeniably harsher than the earlier D7, they do have the 50mph performance necessary for modern traffic. In the metal, the tell-tale signs indicating a B175 are a cylinder head with the sparking plug in the centre, rather than towards the rear as on the previous models, and front forks with hard chrome bottom ends to their legs (not their sliders - check out the picture on p.63) beneath rubber gaiters. Since both these features can be retro-fitted to other models, however, details of late 175 engine and frame numbering have been included at the end of the chapter.

Despite the last one being judged the true 'practical' Bantam, a fairly detailed development history of the model follows, both to put the final one in perspective, and because almost any Bantam is worth having at a pinch, for different requirements. The 125s, for instance, are learner-legal (though there is a modern alternative, found detailed in the final section). 150s are comparatively rare and little different in performance from a 125, but early 175s from 1959 on do carry the improved brakes, and while undergunned for town traffic and burdened with the 3-speed box, if you come on a good-running example, it can still provide a useful tool for country riding (if a particular bike was going to succumb to crank breakage, it would probably have done so in the 30-odd years since it was made). Likewise, the '68 D14/4s and their exploding rivets. But if there is any choice, go for a B175.

Bantam Development History

Here is a short, technical description of the model, followed by a year-by-year development. As in the rest of the book, all dates refer to the production year, even though this may actually have commenced in September of the previous year; so a machine built in, say, November 1951 will be referred to, as it was by the manufacturers, as a 1952 model.

1948/9

The basic D1 engine as seen late in 1948 was a 123cc unit with a bore and stroke of 52 x 58mm. (The stroke, and hence the engine height, would never vary, and since the engine fixing points also never changed, any Bantam engine will fit in any Bantam frame, a useful piece of information if you want to insert a 125, to learn on, into later cycle parts.) It had an alloy head (and always would, despite what the Pitmans book says about iron ones!), with 13 vertical fins running fore and aft, and the spark plug position lying backwards on the centre line. Beneath was a slim, waisted iron barrel, tilting slightly forward and black-painted like almost all Bantams, with 10 horizontal fins styled to match the head. The egg-shaped crankcases were split on the vertical line. Inside them ran a pair of substantial full-circle flywheels with balance weights forged into them but completely encircled by the outer flywheel rim; the hollows formed ... the flywheel were enclosed by thin steel discs retained in a recess in the flywheel side by centre punching.

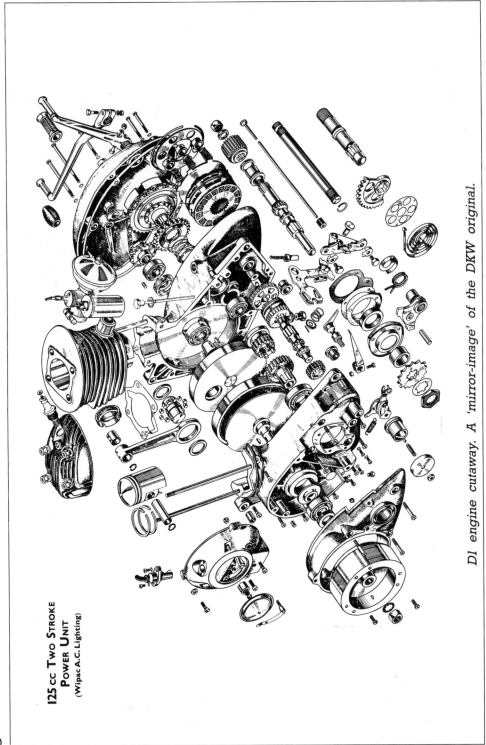

125cc Two Stroke Power Unit
(Wipac A.C. Lighting)

D1 engine cutaway. A 'mirror-image' of the DKW original.

The way they were. A 1961 plunger GPO Bantam well enough restored to take the Cockerel Trophy in 1986 for owner Peggy Clarke. 19

The flywheels ran on pressed-in shafts, and the big-end was pressed into them also. This crankshaft assembly ran on three ball main bearings, two on the drive side, which on the Bantam was on the right, and a single one on the left. Those bearings' dimensions never changed. The big-end ran on a single row of uncaged rollers directly in the eye of the con-rod, which was a steel stamping with a phosphor bronze small end bush; a hollow gudgeon pin ran in the latter. The piston had a slightly domed crown giving 6.5:1 compression, with two pegged rings and a cutaway below the gudgeon pin on each side to assist a free flow of mixture into the transfer ports.

The cylinder barrel's exhaust port was on the right, and threaded externally to take an exhaust pipe nut. At the rear, the inlet port was a short, horizontal stub to carry a clip-fitting $\frac{5}{8}$ in Amal carburettor and its circular wire-mesh air cleaner. This incorporated a 'strangler' choke, operated by moving a knob sideways to close off the wire mesh. Within the barrel, there was a Schnurle loop-type transfer port at 180° on each side of the engine, positioned on the crankshaft axis to match passages angled so that the mixture was directed to the rear of the cylinder. Oil recesses at the bottom of the transfer passages fed oilways drilled to lubricate the inner two main bearings, as the crankcase seals lay outboard of the left side main and of the inner right side one, with lubrication from the outer drive main taken care of by the gearbox oil, which should therefore be checked regularly. (This was an improvement on the early prototypes, which had **41** carried the seal inboard of the left-hand bearing, leaving it completely unlubricated!)

On the left end of the crankshaft, a Wico-Pacy (Wipac) magneto generator, known as the Geni-Mag, had a heavy permanent magnet rotor flywheel keyed and bolted to the crankshaft.

A casting surrounding the rotor had clamped to it the stator plate with the ignition and lighting coils, and with the ignition points housed on its outside. They were readily accessible behind a small circular plate retained by a single sprung metal arm. Outboard of the rotor a pre-oiled bush further supported the crankshaft, and the ignition cam was keyed to the end of the crankshaft. This casting also carried the clutch lifting mechanism. The HT lead ran straight out of the top of the casting to the plug cap, and lighting was direct, with the pilot light powered by a dry cell carried in the headlamp, and the switch a four position thumb-operated one like an air lever, working a cable and mounted on the handlebar. With this system the lights only operated when the engine was running.

On the right, primary drive was by a single row chain with no tensioner. The 6-spring 3-plate clutch ran on a bronze bush. It was operated by a mechanism situated to the rear of the generator set. The clutch cable pulled a lever which turned a 3-start, quick thread worm with a hardened adjustable screw at its centre which could be adjusted from outside the engine, on the left crankcase cover. The 3-speed gearbox was unusual in featuring a crossover drive from

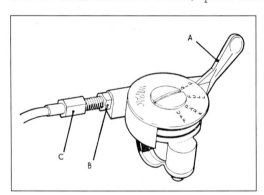

Dl's handlebar-mounted thumb-operated light switch.

A.Switch Lever
B.Lock-nut
C.Adjuster for synchronizing

the clutch on the right to the sprocket on the left. The layshaft was 'normally' positioned below the mainshaft however, and on the latter ran the output mainshaft carrying the 15-tooth gearbox sprocket. Ball races supported the mainshaft, bushes the layshaft and the sleeve gear. The two centre gears were linked and moved together restrained by a positive stop mechanism. The gearchange return spring was located there.

The shaft for the gear pedal ran through the centre of the kickstarter shaft in concentric fashion. The gear pedal shaft carried a quadrant gear which meshed with a ratchet gear engaging with the back of the clutch, which unusually for British machines at that time gave primary kickstarting, with the whole mechanism contained behind the oiltight egg-shaped right-hand cover. A gear position indicator came out on the left with the numbers indicated by a transfer on the top of the rear chainguard. Passages between **42** the primary drive and gearbox meant that lubrication for them was in common, being ¾ pint put in through a filler hole in the right side top of the crankcase, with the hole's plug carrying a dipstick.

The engine was slotted into a simple all-welded loop frame with a single down tube and a rigid rear end. Wheels were fitted with 2.75 x 19in tyres and 5in diameter half-width brakes. Wheelbase was 50in, some 6in more compact than 'ordinary' motorcycles of the time. The sprung telescopic front forks were undamped and non-hydraulic, sliding on grease-lubricated bronze bushes. The frame was fitted with a spring-up centre stand fastened by a clip, a massively valanced front mudguard fastened to the fixed fork tubes, which bore the front number on its sides, a rear carrier which also supported the very full rear mudguard with its tapering valance, adjustable handlebars with the pivot blocks welded on, a D-shaped speedometer and a rectangular toolbox on the right side. A further prominent feature was the bulb horn, ingeniously mounted vertically on top of the forks so that it worked through the steering head stem to the flared mouthpiece screwed into the bottom. A sprung saddle and the pear-shaped 'flat' silencer, with the exhaust pipe first passing beneath the right-hand

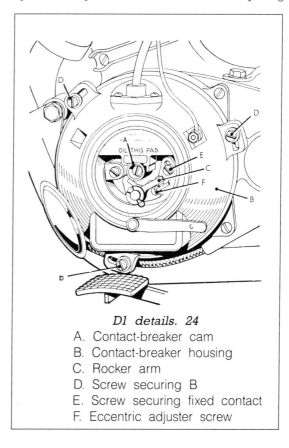

D1 details. 24

A. Contact-breaker cam
B. Contact-breaker housing
C. Rocker arm
D. Screw securing B
E. Screw securing fixed contact
F. Eccentric adjuster screw

footrest, completed the picture, together with an all-over finish of Mist Green, including the wheel rims. This colour was set off by the cream yellow side panels of the gracefully swelling petrol tank. The side panel's shape was set off by both an external gold and internal maroon pinstripe, but for this first year it carried the winged 'BSA' logo in maroon, rather than the later definitive Bantam cockerel. The same winged BSA logo was cast into the right-hand crankcase cover. A 47mph absolute top speed, 128 miles to the gallon, and a £60 price were the vital statistics.

Remarks

The design was very nearly right from the start, though where there were faults, they did, in some cases, linger on. On a practical level, cold starting 43

44 D1 Bantam for its first year.

was never easy and required a fully closed 'strangler' and a well-flooded carb. The concentric layout of the kickstart and gearchange meant that the kickstart pedal dug into the back of your thigh; a folding kick start off the Competition or the D10-D14/4 Sports models is a benefit. The gear lever was exceptionally long and meant the right foot coming off the rest to hook under it and move it up, and on the other side the rear brake pedal was similarly high set. This would remain so until the end.

Furthermore, the gearshift and kickstart were located on rather weak serrations on the shaft, and had to be tightened regularly or they stripped. The three gears were widely spaced, with big gaps between them. This suggested a slight overgearing of the top two, and aggravated another trait encouraged by both the engine's docility and its non-enthusiast riders' moderate style — low engine speeds meant low engine temperature. This could encourage condensation in the crankcase, which together with the minimal main bearing oiling, could lead to the main bearings being attacked by rust. Another lubrication irritant concerned the awkwardly narrow, angled gearbox filler hole in the top of the crankcase, though this problem is easily overcome with a small plastic funnel. Of the cycle parts, the centre stand proved very prone to rapid wear, both of the stand itself and the frame lugs that carried it, followed by collapse. The early clip fitting was an additional hazard. The optional prop stand was and remained to the end a highly desirable extra. Finally, the engine's modest power output meant that vibration was also moderate.

Internally, main bearing lubrication was at first only just adequate. The famous gearchange return spring was positioned in such a way that if it broke, the crankcase had to be split to replace it. In the flywheels, the thin steel discs enclosing the hollows formed in the wheels sometimes worked loose, so that they continued to revolve after the engine had stopped! Wipac electrics were an economy option in general standing below Lucas but above Miller in the scheme of things, and this was reflected in comparatively quick-wear points, and later in the wiring and switches. The ignition cam being keyed to the end of the crankshaft naturally meant that any wear in the main bearings, or in the bronze bush outboard of the rotor, would put the ignition timing out. If the engine will only run with a points gap less than the recommended 0.015in, this could indicate that rotor magnetism has become low; it can be remagnetised by a specialist. But the system was simple enough, and when in good condition worked adequately, certainly by contemporary standards.

1950

A number of changes in specification came into effect this year, which comprised the option of alternative battery-powered electrics using a Lucas 1A45 generator and rectifier to permit the fitting of a stop light, electric horn and a headlamp-mounted ignition switch. In consequence, models so equipped had a different left-hand crankcase cover and toolbox. On these battery models the crankshaft itself was shorter and the flywheels had thicker 45 rims. Another option was that of plunger-type rear suspension, which gave 2 to 3in of rear wheel movement. The plunger models were fitted with a new rear mudguard, with a differently-shaped valance running its full length. It was this year that the competition models made their debut.

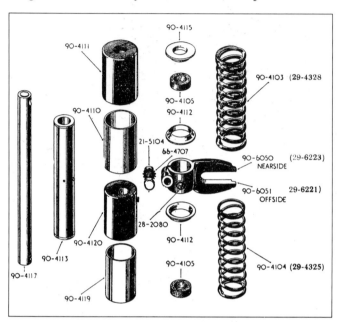

The elements of BSA's simple plunger rear springing.

Modifications to the roadster models related to the centre stand spring, the fitting of corrugated gaiters to the lower ends of the front fork assembly, a different saddle, and from engine number YD24813, the use of an exhaust pipe and silencer that ran above the right-hand footrest.

Competition D1 in action in the 80s with Rowland Clarke of the Bantam Owners Club negotiating a section during the 1985 Arbuthnot Trial.

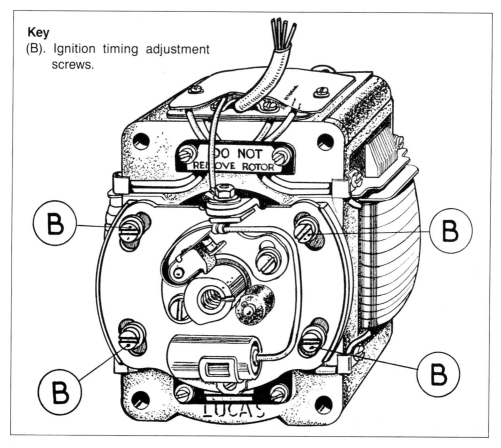

Key
(B). Ignition timing adjustment
screws.

Lucas generator 1A45 introduced in 1950 for 'battery' models.

Remarks

In practice, and despite their extra cost, dealers who had to tackle the Lucas battery models were not impressed by the system's performance. They were a marked improvement, however, on their Geni-Mag counterparts, and were a little faster as their generator rotors were lighter.

1951

From engine number YD40661, the Wipac Geni-Mag was replaced by a later but similar version known as the SS55/Mk8, identified by having a larger coverplate retained by two screws and with a cast-in winged BSA logo. The HT lead was now soldered directly to the internal ignition coil and emerged to the rear of its original location. An Amal Type 361/1 carburettor was now specified and the front fork bushes became detachable.

Remarks

The new Wipac electrics were easier to service than those of the previous Geni-Mag and were considerably more efficient. They did, however, have **47** a common fault according to Roy Bacon, who was much involved with racing Bantams. The pin on which the moving contact breaker arm pivoted could work loose in its baseplate, producing wide variations in timing and a bike that would either start quickly or run, but not both. Cures vary, from fabricating a new pin which screws into the baseplate and using Loctite to retain it in place, or, being careful to use the appropriate puller, removing the stator armature carrying the coils and cutting away some of the casting to provide additional space for an extra locknut for the new pin.

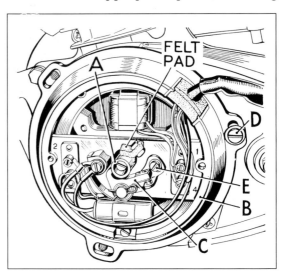

Wipac S55/Mk 8 generator, introduced for 'direct' models from 1951 on.

A. Contact-breaker cam
B. Contact-breaker housing
C. Rocker arm
D. Screw securing B
E. Screw securing fixed contact

In addition, the fit of the stator on its mounting also needs to be checked, as this determines the air gap between it and the rotor. If, as often is the case, the stator fit is poor, the rotor location, which in turn depends on the crankshaft being exactly in line, becomes critical. Overall, the system proved itself adequate, even though lighting was always on the feeble side.

1952

Changes for this year were limited to the use of stronger headstock gussets, rear frame stays of thicker tubing, improved front wheel spindle material and the fitting of a headlamp switch to the direct lighting models.

1953

1953 marked the production of the 100,000th D1 model. An optional black finish now became available and all models were supplied with chrome-plated wheel rims. Engine changes comprised increasing the number of uncaged big-end rollers from 12 to 14 and increasing their length from 7mm to $\frac{3}{8}$in, the flywheels being recessed to suit and the connecting rod broadened. The number of screws holding the crankcase halves together were increased from 11 to 13, one now being fitted behind the clutch on the right-hand side.

The front mudguard was now unsprung and of a more shallow and shapely profile. A dualseat was optional; when fitted, extra mudguard stays were needed, as previously the carrier had supported the rear mudguard.

The engine number was now stamped on the top of the crankcase, to the rear of the cylinder barrel, and no longer on the front mounting lug.

1954

The 148cc D3 Bantam Major now made its debut, as a result of increasing the bore size of the D1 cylinder barrel from 52 to 58mm. It was finished in pastel grey but retained the cream and yellow tank panels. Both the newcomer and the existing D1 model now had a broader cylinder barrel with more generous finning, the original spigot and crankcase stud centres being retained. A new base gasket was now required. The profile and finning of the cylinder head were also changed to match, and a cylinder head gasket fitted.

Internally, the size of the transfer ports was increased and all flywheels were now of the thicker type used previously when Lucas lighting equipment had been specified. The drive-side (right-hand) crankcase seal, previously located between the two drive-side main bearings, was moved inboard of both bearings and relocated against the flywheel, which now had a rubbing diameter to suit. The left-hand seal was moved 0.010in further outboard, the crankshaft being extended by that amount. An oilway drilling

1955 148cc D3 Major.

was introduced to channel lubricant to the left-hand bearing, with a catchment area filled by primary chaincase oil and a drainway. A word of caution is necessary here as some early broad-barrelled D1 models may have been fitted with earlier crankshaft to use up existing stocks.

The new D3 Bantam Major was fitted with a more substantial front fork assembly, derived from the 1954 C10L model. All Bantam forks now incorporated the synthetic rubber inserts used to provide damping that had been fitted previously only to the Competition models. The D3 and the Competition models from now on featured a headlamp cowl, the D1 model fitting a special version that required modified fork yokes. All models were now fitted with a tubular silencer having a detachable finned tail, to replace the original flat pear-shaped design. For plunger models the rear wheel hub was changed to take a larger diameter spindle. All petrol tanks were fitted with chrome plated beads over their two raised seams. On battery lighting models only, the toolbox was transferred to the left-hand side.

1955

This year only minor modifications were made which comprised enlarging the size of the cylinder barrel spigot and increasing the stud centres to 55mm. The design of the optional dualseat was changed and the profile of the rear number plate altered.

1956

The rigid frame D1 and Competition models were discontinued, and for the D3 model swinging arm rear suspension became available, with a bolted-on sub-frame attached to a modified front loop. The swinging arm assembly pivoted on Silentbloc bushes and was controlled by non-adjustable rear suspension units with $10\frac{1}{2}$ inch centre-to-centre measurements, later changed to $11\frac{1}{2}$ inch which remained unchanged to the end of production. Side panels held by a single screw fastening were of the A10 type, triangular in shape. An optional steering lock became available.

Other modifications comprised a new and shorter exhaust pipe with a longer tail fin silencer, the latter having a recessed area to clear the right-hand suspension unit. A new, stepped dualseat was introduced, although the option of a saddle remained using a modified version of the original D1 type. The rear brake backplate contained a revised location slot and the rear chainguard was fitted with a small extension piece. The fuel tank filler cap was transferred to the offside, to prevent neat oil going straight into the left-hand mounted petrol tap. The gearchange indicator was, apparently, deleted.

Mid-year a further modification was made, to the engine. Having deleted the spacing collar between the flywheel and the main bearing when the stud centres were widened, there was a need to replace it by an oil drag fan to create turbulence for the incoming mixture. Engines with DD and DDB prefixes should have shims fitted to the left-hand side only, in consequence.

Remarks

The swinging arm D3's handling was good, with only the low-set footrests inhibiting bend swinging, its appearance having been neatened for a weight penalty of 20lb, to give a dry weight of 216lb. The seat height had been increased to 30 inches but the overall narrowness meant that most riders could still touch the ground with both feet. The new exhaust system led to a noticeable improvement in performance, but at the expense of more noise.

1957

For the D1 and D3 models (and the following year's new D5 model) the left-hand crankshaft seal was repositioned inboard of the left-hand main

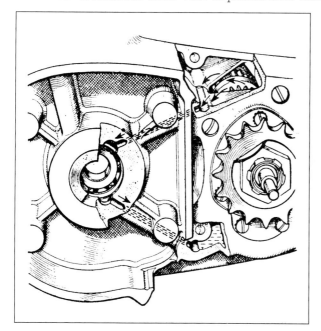

bearing, with a rubbing diameter on the flywheel. An extra seal was also fitted. A collection area for lubricant to be fed to the left-hand main bearing was added, oil being supplied from the gearbox with an appropriate drain hole.

Mid-1957-on revision to the 150 and the 175 models' lubrication.

Remarks

These measures succeeded in overcoming the problems of main bearing lubrication, which previously had relied upon only a residue of oil running down an oil hole. On stripping an engine, the main bearings would inevitably be black coloured, as the result of burning from blow-back. The new sealing arrangements certainly improved the life of the main bearings, but as the oil seals began to deteriorate, gearbox oil would be sucked in, resulting in a very smoky exhaust.

1958

Production of the 150cc D3 model ceased, due to the introduction of a bored-out version, the 7.4bhp 172cc D5. Finished in maroon, with oval, ivory panels on a rounded, larger (2 gallon) petrol tank with only a single seam, the basic engine design had again received some further attention. With the crankcase studs now set at 60mm to accommodate the increased bore size of 61.5mm, the big-end contained a caged roller bearing assembly, **51** the connecting rod incorporating radial drillings. A flat top piston with two 3/32 inch width rings raised the compression ratio to 7.4:1. An Amal Monobloc carburettor bolted to the cylinder barrel, abandoning the earlier clip-fitting arrangement. The gearing was modified by fitting a 16 tooth gearbox sprocket (previously 17 tooth) and a rear wheel sprocket of 46 teeth (previously 47 tooth). Attention to the clutch necessitated a change to the friction plates, with bonded-on material in place of cork.

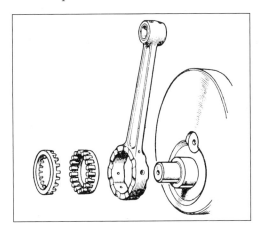

Reverting to the D5 cycle parts, the brake diameter remained at 5 inches but the width of both sets of shoes was increased to 0.87in.

Caged roller big end introduced for 1958 on.

The rear brakeplate location slot was altered to suit. A new rear chainguard had an additional bracket half way along the top. Both wheels were of 3.00 x 18in. size, the front one having a new, wider 36 spoke hub. The front fork assembly was modified internally and handlebars of the C10L type fitted. The dualseat shape was again revised and changes made to the silencer, which was provided with a single bolt attachment bracket.

The D1 model was now available with the option of a maroon finish.

52 *D7 Super 175, this one from 1961.*

1959

This year marked the introduction of the 172cc D7 Super model, finished in royal red and ivory with a light coloured dualseat, although there was the option of a black and ivory version. Externally, the left-hand crankcase had a smoother finish and the word 'Super' cast into it, the clutch adjustment screw now being relocated on the inside. Internally, the piston was now fitted with three 3/32 in wide piston rings and had a modified gudgeon pin and circlips. An extra set of splines that had been added previously to the gearbox mainshaft and layshaft were deleted, the selector 'flag' on the gearchange ratchet plate made more substantial and the slot for second gear selection deepened.

As regards the cycle parts, the brake drums were now enlarged to 5½in diameter and the width increased to a full 1in. A new front fork assembly was fitted, similar to that of the Triumph Tiger Cub but shorter, using C15 headrace cups and cones. A new fixed nacelle came into use, with a round speedometer and new switches. At the rear end the trapped tubing ends of the swinging arm fork were changed to solid, the rear fork pivot having a pressed-in pivot pin mounted on bronze bushes. The rear brake torque arm was now attached to a clip on the swinging arm's left leg. The rear wheel hub took the form of the cast iron type specified for the Triumph Tiger Cub, with a bolt-on sprocket. The brake backplate utilised a longer torque arm with a slot in its forward end for an anchor bolt.

The sub-frame now had a seat loop with two support tubes, the front portion being changed to suit the new fork pivot and new footrests (now common to all models, except the trail version of the D7). The silencer reverted to its original position, passing under the right-hand footrest. Matching C15-type side and centre panels were used, fastened by hollow bolts registering over threaded pillars, the right-hand toolbox fitting around

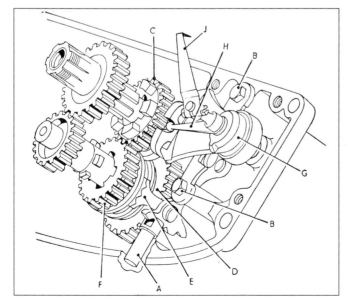

Early Bantam 3-speed gearbox mechanism, sometimes overstressed when revised in 175s. 35

A. Spring-loaded plunger
B. Bolts securing selector-mechanism
C. Mainshaft sliding gear
D. Layshaft first gear
E. Gear-selector arm
F. Layshaft second gear
G. Foot gear-change pedal shaft spring and spring loaded claw assembly
H. Gear-postion indicator lever

the inner panel and matching the centre one.

Other modifications comprised a new centre stand, dualseat, rear chainguard, handlebar bend (now raised), silencer and rear brake rod. All 175cc wheel rims were of the 40 hole type from now on.

Remarks

The D7 represented the parting of the ways with the D1, which soldiered on in plunger form with the old forks and still with direct or battery lighting option, like the D7. The increased power of the D7 was welcome, but the deletion of the additional splines on the three-speed gearbox was a retrograde step and also one that poses problems during a rebuild, as the earlier and later gear assemblies are not interchangeable. The change had been made in the interests of production economy since without the additonal splines the gears no longer needed to be hollow. With nearly double the D1's power output applied to a weaker version of the original D1 gearbox, jumping out of gear, particularly second gear, became a serious problem until 1967. Ironically, the modifications made to the ratchet plate described earlier were addressed at this problem of jumping out of second gear, which on the D1 model was due to the somewhat insubstantial selector flag riveted to the ratchet plate quickly becoming a floppy fit. A temporary cure had been to tighten the flag by hitting the rivet that secured it, or as the Bantam racers did, by doubling up the number of circlips underneath the spring that held the two halves of the selector itself together, tightening it up.

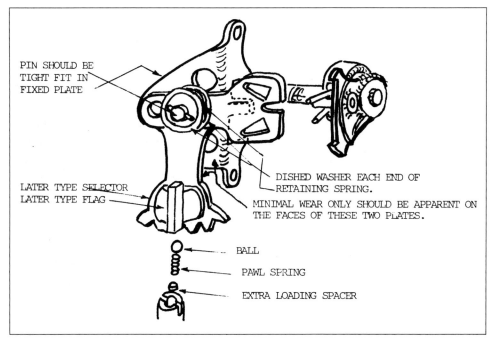

54 *Bantam Racing Club's mods for three speed gearbox.*

The additional power sometimes over-stressed the Woodruff key on the crankshaft, its size having remained unaltered. Fracture occurred around the key and then the whole shaft would snap, with a distinctive sound, taking the flywheel with it.

The D7's bulkier looks, which tended to dwarf the shapely engine, were not to everyone's taste, and some of the features were counter-productive. The fastenings on the D7's new side panels were fiendishly difficult to do up again, having to be located blind on their pillars, twice. Access to the battery meant loosening off the bolts on the top of the suspension units to permit removal of the seat. The centre stand was not much of an improvement either. Yet the new frame's handling was respectable and one enormous benefit were the brakes, which had reached their final form and were really efficient. Weight had climbed to its 224lb peak but even if power had increased it was still of the tractable, docile sort, as a top speed in the mid-fifties indicated, but with good power low down the rev band. For the next seven years, changes would be mainly cosmetic.

1960

The Dls frame, fork and headlamp were now finished in black. On the D7, the frame had an added lug for padlocking the steering.

1961

The petrol tank of the D7 now featured pear-shaped badges and could be obtained with optional gold-lined chrome side panels. An optional finish for the complete machine in sapphire blue became available too.

1962

The D7 engine had its small end bearing modified to accept a Torrington needle race, and the crankcase was modified to feature three extra fixing screws, one under the top rear-mounting bolt hole. The ratios of the three-speed gearbox were revised and the layshaft altered, changes to the splines on the gear shafts affecting the sliding pinions. The size of the rear sprocket was increased to 47 teeth and a new type of silencer was fitted, retained by two bolts. The front mudguard clip now featured two fixing holes and the rear mudguard design was revised, with the option of a grab rail. A new rear number plate had the tail light attached to the top of it and the left-hand side panel, battery carrier and rear chainguard were modified, the last two to their final form. Pillion footrests were standardised throughout the range and the handlebar bend again revised, with the option of a higher rise one like that fitted to the 1967 C25 model.

1963

This year marked the end of the D1 model.

1964

The only changes that took place this year related to the speedometer, which was changed to one of the magnetic type, a further modification to the silencer and another modification to the big-end assembly to improve lubrication.

1965

This year saw the introduction of the D7 de luxe model with its kidney-shaped 1.95 gallon petrol tank having twin top seams with chrome-plated beads, a central filler cap and an oval-shaped chrome-plated side area fitted with circular plastic badges. It was finished in Flamboyant Red with white pinstriping on the mudguard valances, and polished crankcase covers. The new torpedo-shaped silencer had a black unfinned end cap and the new black dualseat had red piping at the front and rear and a grab-strap with visible metal attachment clips. Ball-ended levers were fitted to new handlebars. The de luxe (battery only) and battery model Super both employed an external ignition coil, which necessitated having an extra ignition switch on the headlamp.

Edward Turner restyling gives a new lease of life. A 1966 D7 de Luxe.

1966

The D7 Super model was discontinued and the D7 de luxe joined by an economy version, the D7 Silver Bantam. The latter was finished in Sapphire Blue, with mudguards, headlamp cowl, and the petrol tank's side panels in polychromatic silver. The dualseat lacked a grab handle and had white piping at the front and rear.

1967

The D7 models were discontinued, to be replaced by the D10 range, which comprised new versions of the Silver Bantam and the Supreme, and two new additions, the four-speed Sports and Bushman models. (Early D10 Supreme models had, in fact, become available as early as July the preceding year). The D10 Supreme was finished in polychromatic blue, its petrol tank having a horizontal 'S' line along its side, starting above the round badge and separating the blue upper from the chrome plated lower section, this line being picked out in white. Two stainless steel mirrors were affixed to the C25-type handlebars, now used on all Bantam roadsters apart from the new Sports model to be described later. The dualseat was in black with white piping and had a grab-strap. A minor modification applied to all models was changing the petrol tank's rear fixing holes to slots. The D10 Silver Bantam was made to the same specification as its D7 predecessor.

The new D10 Sports model also had a polychromatic finish, with chequered tape on the tank top. Its specification closely followed that of the Supreme but differed in having a flyscreen bearing the front registration numbers, a seat with a hump at its tail and a chrome plated strip along its edges, chrome plated mudguards and a separate, chrome plated headlamp shell with a main beam warning light. The exhaust system was high level, with twin chrome heatshields of oval shape, and the wheel hubs were of the full-width type. Exposed springs on the rear suspension units, a folding kickstart, rectangular rear number plate, single point rear lamp and flat handlebars completed the specification.

The D10 Bushman was intended as a cross-country machine and therefore had a different, raised frame and side panels, with a bash plate, 58 tooth rear sprocket, high-level exhaust system, separate headlamp with only one switch as an energy transfer ignition system was used, a single point rear lamp, 66-70 B44-type handlebars and an air filter mounted behind the right-hand side panel. It was finished in orange and white.

All models now used a new crankshaft, which had a parallel-sided left-hand end to accept the rotor of a Wipac 60 watt six coil alternator that supplied current through a metal plate rectifier. The size of the Woodruff key was now reduced, to minimise a stress point. The right-hand end of the crankshaft had been extended so that it would pass through the primary chaincase and carry an ignition timing cam. This operated contact breaker points, now sited behind a new, circular, fluted cover on the right-hand crankcase cover. Headlamp bulbs could now be uprated from 24/24 watt to 24/30 watt.

All engines had an increase in compression ratio to 8.65:1, brought about by a domed piston with two $\frac{1}{16}$ inch wide rings, fitted to a new oval section connecting rod and a new cylinder head with an increased squish band, the last requiring yet another (and final) head gasket. Discs attached to the flywheels increased primary compression. The cylinder barrel porting was modified and the crankcase was provided with an extra dowel hole on the right. The left-hand crankcase cover featured a flute to replace the previous 'Super' casting.

The three-speed gearbox returned to its earlier design, with two sets of splines on the mainshaft and layshaft. The clutch now comprised four friction and three plain plates and had a new hub centre and a modified **57**

1967 D10 Supreme.

1967 D10 Silver Bantam, an economy option.

Complete with chequered sticky-tape, the 1967 D10 Sports.

chainwheel (with a variant for the D10 Bushman). The engine sprocket was modified by having its rear counter-bored to accept an 'O' ring to seal off the points. The adoption of a Type 626 Amal Concentric carburettor necessitated a handlebar-mounted air lever in place of the earlier strangler and it was fitted with a pancake type air filter comprising a paper element in a chrome plated, perforated drum. Footrest and pillion footrest rubbers now conformed to those used on the rest of the BSA range.

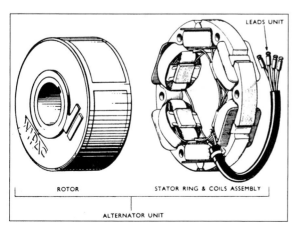

New Wipac alternator for 1967.

Remarks

The D10s were a mixed blessing. With higher compression, increased performance became a reality, but as with four stroke singles and twins, harshness and vibration were increased too. This was now bad enough to loosen off nuts and bolts and in some cases cause fractures, specifically to the engine front mountings, as well as posing a threat to the new electrics. The alternator itself improved performance, making the engine easier to rev due to its smaller rotor having less flywheel effect. But the electrics, however, posed some problems of their own. A spaghetti-like wiring loom, cheap switches (though they did have the benefit of being identical - and therefore interchangeable - if the ignition switch packed up) and inadequate voltage control, all contributed their share of problems. Extended running without lights could easily mean boiled batteries, as I once found to my cost in Greece. The three-speed gearbox, despite its improvements, was stressed from the increased power, but right from the start there was rarely trouble with the four-speed version. The engine, however, could successfully withstand the increased power.

1968

The D10 series came to an end in 1967 and was replaced by the D14/4 series, the final digit after the oblique stroke indicating all models now had a four-speed gearbox. Only three model variants now comprised the range, the Silver Bantam having been dropped. All were fitted with an engine that had a 10:1 compression ratio via flywheels that were fitted with fatter compression discs retained by rivets. The cylinder head had a redesigned combustion chamber, and the cylinder wider transfer ports and deeper inlet ports. The exhaust pipe diameter was now increased from $1\frac{1}{4}$ in to $1\frac{3}{8}$ in with an adaptor that screwed into the cylinder head's threaded exhaust port. The silencer's open end was enlarged to suit. The left-hand crankcase now had its fixing screws increased from 3 to 4, and a rubber bung provided access to the clutch adjuster. A large Victor Enduro-type paper element air filter was fitted behind the right-hand side cover, retained by a rubber band and attached to the carburettor by a rubber hose. The centre panel had been deleted and the left-hand cover now contained a large hole for access to the battery. The side covers were retained by half turn fasteners.

The D14/4 Supreme was finished in black, with the option of white pinstriping on mudguards and the side panels. It also had a separate, black painted headlamp shell and a new seat with a marble top finish, white piping, a grab-strap and a chrome strip around its base. The petrol tank decoration now comprised a painted portion that commenced below the badge and snaked upwards.

The D14/4 Sports model retained much of the 1967 D10 styling, adopting new cosmetics but having as its exhaust heat shield a single curved component. It now used a Bushman-type front frame section and had a new front mudguard with a new front number plate. A heavier C12-type front fork was fitted with thicker stanchions, each leg having a welded-on mudguard stay and clipless rubber gaiters. The front brake backplate had an anchor arm riveted to it which located with a lug cast in the fork leg.

The Bushman model used the same front fork as the Sports model, had full-width hubs and a seat similar to that of the Supreme.

Remarks

Once again the Bantam's engine could accept the increase in power, with the exception of those that shed the rivets attaching the compression discs to the flywheels. They self-destructed in a major way, which happened frequently enough to create a warranty problem. Small end failures also occurred. A D14/4 on test registered 70mph, although the speedometer error reduced this to a true 66mph, with a 'comfortable' cruising speed said to be an indicated 60mph though 50 was truer in my experience, due to the shakes. At that speed around 80mpg was returned. Acceleration took place in a fairly narrow band ('not quite the low speed slogger it used to be' as *The Motor Cycle* test put it), cutting in rather abruptly and being good up to 50, where it flattened out very noticeably. The new and larger exhaust gave a rather deep and throaty note. On the practical side, the new side panel fasteners were very welcome, but the battery access was a non-starter; the hole was too small, the battery leads too short and other wires running across the hole virtually sealed it off.

1969

The D14/4 Supreme ran from October 1968 (engine number D14C 11333) until April 1969, the Sports and Bushman models being discontinued in October. Thereafter, the sole remaining model was known as the D175 Bantam. Finished in polychromatic red, blue or all-black, the blue mudguards were no longer picked out in white although the red side panels were. Engine-wise, the compression discs were now fastened to the flywheels by a rolled-in rim lock, the whole assembly having a stiffer crankshaft with increased crankpin diameters. The diameter of the gudgeon pin and the small end bearing were changed, as were the piston's circlips. Unified threads were specified in several instances such as the carburettor attachment studs, some frame fasteners and the seat fixing, etc. The crankcase fixing screws were increased to 17 and the left-hand crankcase forward location dowel was made hollow. The cylinder head had a centrally-mounted spark plug, but was interchangeable with the earlier D14 type. The kickstart spindle was enlarged and the clutch chainwheel redesigned. The clutch springs were altered, as was the housing for the contact breaker points.

A new front fork assembly was adopted. The fork was of the Triumph 'Sports Cub' type, slimmer than that of the 1968 Sports model but distinguished by the hard chrome bottom end to the stanchions. It carried a new type of mudguard stay lug. New mudguards, front and rear, were fitted, the front having a bridge support that formed part of the whole assembly. The silencer mounting bracket was changed, a new left-hand 61 side cover fitted and the rear suspension units springs left exposed. The wheels had offset hubs, retaining the Sports-type front brake backplate but with detail revision of the rear brake torque arm. An oil measuring cup no longer formed part of the petrol filler. A main beam warning light was no longer fitted and the main jet of the Amal Concentric carburettor was changed in size to 180.

Above: *D175B Bushman for 1969.*

Below: *Last and best, the B175 Bantam for 1969. A flamboyant red or black model from the pinstriping on its side-panels, this one is also fitted with proprietary Motoplas pannier frames.*

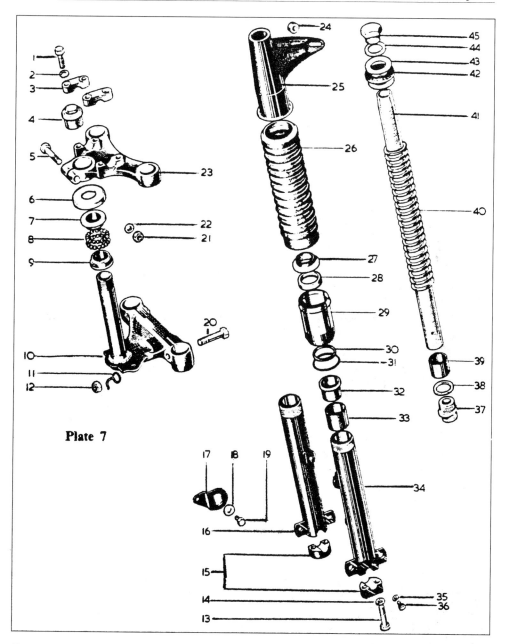

Plate 7

Details of B175 front forks.

Remarks

The B175 model, as it was eventually known, continued unchanged until the end of production during March 1971. Some problems, such as that of charge control, remained, but with the stronger engine and front fork assembly, the B175 could be both pushed along and thrown about with **63** greater confidence than previously. In addition, a combination of increased power and the four-speed box made both two-up riding and tackling hills less problematic. In my opinion, this is the one to own.

Bantams Today

If you choose one of the many second-hand Bantams on the market, buying privately today (1989) you can expect to pay from £150-£300 for a tidy, running 175cc example, and from £75 for a more or less complete non-runner. Prices for Dls are complicated by a tinge of 'collectability', and can be £50-£100 up on the later models. With Dl/D3s, it is important to find one with all the panels and mudguards present, even if they're in poor condition, as these parts are now very scarce.

For the learner, perhaps a late Dl? This is the 1962 version.

Naturally, you cannot expect a totally accurate milometer reading, but bearing general condition in mind, 40-45,000 miles can reasonably be expected from a Bantam engine that is not grossly abused, before major mechanical attention becomes necessary. Even then, it need not be too crippling — a complete engine rebuild with everything renewed currently costs around £250 at specialists T and G.

If you are accustomed to other two-strokes, and especially to modern ones, the Bantam will seem slow-revving, both in terms of its typically two-stroke 'Bim-bam-bim' erratic idling, and of the way in which its acceleration from a standstill comes at its own not very startling speed until the power band is reached — remember we are talking 0-60 in 24 seconds . . . despatching in London, I would often be beaten away from the traffic lights by keen types of 10-speed racing bicycles, though I would usually gain a low revenge when I passed them shortly, since my B175's exhaust was on the smoky side . . . with a four-speed, it's from 20 to 45mph in 3rd and top where some satisfying tunes can be played.

The clutch also feels as if it's doing things in its own time, as the quick thread worm within it rarely fits that well, but though feeling worn and engaging late, it is extremely tough and rarely a source of trouble, working best if the mechanism is kept well greased. This engagement should be clean enough for you to be able to pull in the lever and kickstart the machine while it's in gear. To achieve this, the two parts of the mechanism must be fitted correctly so that the outer is lined up with the casting face and the inner with the cable. Likewise with the four-speed box, finding neutral at a standstill should be no problem. The single row primary chain is nonadjustable but slow to wear — it's due for replacement when up-and-down movement exceeds $\frac{3}{4}$ inch.

Great expectations about Bantam handling will be disappointing - I have read it described as good or even excellent, but I can only wonder what the writers in question had been riding before. 'Adequate' seems truer to me — it's only bolted together after all — with the rather tall (latterly 31in) and narrow swinging-arm frame reinforcing the impression of a motorised bicycle, something which intrinsically prefers to stay upright than be heeled over. On the other hand, the bottom line has to be that over many years I now realise that I have never actually fallen off a Bantam. 'Very adequate'?

Starting, as mentioned, can be a problem, and your best aid here is a good supply of the right spark plugs — Champion N4/NGK B7ES for the late 175s — don't leave home without a clean spare, and a plug spanner, preferably the kind with a short body welded at right angles to a lever, as these are light and simple enough to slip in the jacket pocket. Another aid to clean starting is getting the mixture right, as well as remembering to a) add petrol before the oil; b) close the petrol tap before you do so, because with the later central filler cap the oil can still plummet straight down into the carburettor and clog up everything hopelessly; and c) give the machine a little shake, self-mixing oil or no. The original mixture recommended was 24:1 with 16:1 while running in, but with today's low-ash oils, a mixture of 30 or 32:1 can be used, dropping to 28 or 25:1 if the big end is suspect. Ignore the filler cap and use the measure on the bottle. Apart from the castor based ones, any modern two-stroke oil will do, and they can be mixed, so that a tankful involving a different oil will do no harm. The less oil, the weaker it runs and the hotter it detonates, so the compromise you are seeking is between that, and clogging it up with too much oil. Bantams, even the high compression ones, run happily on 2 star petrol, which suggests very strongly that unleaded will do too, but there is no definite information on this yet; once again, the occasional switch to 4 star will not damage the engine.

A might-have-been. Umberslade Hall stylist Steve Mettam in 1970 with a projected trail version of the B175 Bushman which never reached production.

If unleaded is used with low-ash oil, a leaner jet in the carb may be necessary to handle the less viscous mixture. Light gear oil, 75 weight, will do for the gearbox. Finally, one more point on starting — a rebuilt Bantam engine **always** has to be push started the first time.

A starting problem may have an electrical source. Whatever the model, gapping the points correctly and if necessary renewing the Wipac coil with a new one is usually the answer. Otherwise, try renewing the ignition switch if one is fitted. While on electrical matters, on battery lighting Dls, the original 2 amp small battery fitted is just about OK for running and the use of a stoplight, but a more modern 10 amp one plus a modern rectifier is really necessary if you are to use the lights regularly. For the Dl direct system, the original dry cell batteries for the pilot light are no longer obtainable. The later model electrics can be erratic. I have had one that began to die every time the stoplight was applied, and in fact when it came to selling the last Bantam I owned, for the first time ever the headlight failed, possibly in protest, in the middle of a lively evening demonstration run with the prospective purchaser, a punk rocker living in a squat in Hackney, perched on the pillion. (He never noticed, and honours ended up even as he never returned the helmet I lent him to get home, and for many months after I sold the bike I was pursued by police enquiries regarding the machine and its rider's behaviour.)

The overcharging and battery boiling syndrome is the worst feature; in Greece, I was glad of the Bantam's light weight, as when it died high

More might-have-beens. Small Heath's own projected 'Budgie' restyled 175 roadster, with, in the foreground, Michael Martin's 250 'Mickmar' development.

in the hills around Delphi, a friendly road-mending gang hoisted it into their truck and gave us both a lift down to the coast, where a new battery got us all the way back to England. The ultimate answer would be a 12-volt conversion with zener diode voltage control, but this would probably be easiest with a late Lucas system. Preliminary explorations by Bantam specialists T and G indicate that one Lucas alternator rotor will bolt directly on in place of the Wipac one; details should be available from them by the time you read this. One day soon, this will become a matter of urgency, as Wipac no longer manufacture or supply motorcycle electrical components, and the supply of flywheel magneto ignition coils is already a problem.

A badly smoking Bantam means either that the mixture is overdoing the oil; or that the silencer needs cleaning out, a nasty job involving caustic soda, rubber gloves, and copious muck; or finally, on post '57 machines, that a crankcase seal is cracked, allowing gearbox oil into the engine. If the machine you acquire has been standing for anything over a year, the crankcase seals will probably have perished and be letting in air as well. The result will be a machine that will not start and when it does, revs wildly, or one that runs for a while and then packs up, or only runs at half throttle, smoking excessively. Renewing the seals is the solution. They cost around £1.50 each, and most bike shops will be able to fit them if you don't feel up to it. If you are working on your own engine, a flywheel extractor and clutch compressor are advisable, and available from T and G at around £10 the pair.

One real plus point when dealing with Bantams is the good interchangeability. Most of the long-run common parts are mentioned in the development history, but here are one or two more. They will all run satisfactorily on each other's exhausts and silencers, except for the '68-on when the length became more critical due to the porting. Even then it can be done. The final drive chain was always ½in, though there were variations in length; a modern 420 size is the suitable alternative. Main bearings, clutch spring cups, the clutch pressure plate and the quick-thread mechanism are all the same, though the latter are shorter on four-speed models. One rear chainguard fits all the roadster 175s from the D7 onwards, despite minor variations. One more interchangeable component is the petrol tank. An old-style tank will fit on any machine, as I know because the near-new B175 which I took to Crete was kitted out with an early D1 tank finished, in a twisted homage to the chopper cult, in spray-can metallic scarlet. On the same theme, the silencer was an early D7 tail-pipe job, bent up at an angle. The result had at least one advantage. It was so, ah, **individual**-looking that when I left the machine in a public parking slot by the water in Venice for five days, I came back to find it completely undisturbed, despite the fixed switches making it all too easy to ride away or at least to drain the battery. It had only been secured with a bicycle chain!. I still think the D1 tanks are pretty. Fitting a later tank is a hellish job, especially due to the chrome strips and the fact that the main electrical earth is secured by one of the attachment bolts.

68 *One to look for, a 1970 B175.*

The major possible interchange, as mentioned, is the engine. People create learner legal bikes by putting D1 engines in D14/4 cycle parts, but many prefer the later machine's more powerful electrics, and for them an alternative now beckons. Andy Tidball at T and G is producing a sleeved-down barrel to convert a 175 to a 125. Cost of the kit is around £75, on an exchange basis, and preliminary reports on performance are encouraging. There is no apparent problem with the DVLC for a machine converted in this way, so long as you inform them and send your V5 document in to be amended, since as mentioned, from their point of view, it is the chassis rather than the engine which constitutes the real vehicle. One minor benefit is road tax reduced from £20 to £10 per annum at current rates.

T and G are good advice-givers (they have certainly helped me with this chapter) and problem-solvers for Bantams (a modern side-stand, substitute speedometers and pistons, etc.) and also a good source of spares — check their 10 page list — with discounts for Bantam Owners Club members. For volume, however, it is hard to compete with the Birmingham shops which benefited from the BSA factory clear-out, starting with the ever-obliging C and D Autos, who also knock 10% off for BSA Owner's Club members. Most BSA specialists will carry some Bantam bits, so it is always worth trying your local British shop first. Armours of Bournemouth supply replica pipes and silencers. For the 125, with its 2.75 x 19in wheel dimensions, K70 Dunlop tyres are suitable at £18.75 each, while for the 175s at 3.00 x 18in, there are Avon Supremes at around £25, or Pirelli Mandrakes, but with a smaller 2.75 equivalent section rather than 3.00 on the front, because a modern profile 3.00 rubs on the mudguard.

On a Bantam, the ever leak-prone fork seals, the lack of a fuel reserve, of a lockable toolbox, and of a qd rear wheel can all be irritating, especially the latter since rear wheel removal is not easy. Changing the clutch cable is peculiar, as the cable end disappears under the left side of the crankcase and has to be located blind (and messily). But the later brakes are good, and the engine and four-speed box were built to last, adding up to a machine that is at least as valid as a Morris Minor on today's roads. So look around for a prop stand, a folding kickstart, a Pitmans handbook, and one of the original pressed steel luggage racks, and then enjoy your Bantam, which with even moderate levels of attention can prove a trusty bird.

BSA Bantam B175 (1970): Technical Data

Engine		Brakes	
Bore, (mm)	61.5	Diam. front, (in)	$5\frac{1}{2}$
Stroke, (mm)	58	Diam. rear, (in)	$5\frac{1}{2}$
Capacity, (cc)	173	**Tyres**	
Compression ratio	9.5:1	Size front, (in)	3.00 x 18
Ignition	coil	Size rear, (in)	3.00 x 18
Carburettor	Amal Concentric		

Transmission			Electrical	
Sprockets			Battery	10ah
			Headlamp (dia. in)	6
Engine	17		Voltage	6
Clutch	38		**Miscellaneous**	
Gearbox	16		Fuel, Imp. (gall).	$1\frac{7}{8}$
Rear wheel	47		Seat height, (in.)	31
Top gear	6.58		Width, (in)	$26\frac{1}{4}$
3rd gear	8.55		Length, (in)	$78\frac{1}{2}$
2nd gear	12.04		Ground clearance	
1st gear	18.68		unladen, (in)	$7\frac{1}{2}$
Chain (front)	$\frac{3}{8}$in x $\frac{1}{4}$in 50 pitches		Dry weight, (lb.)	216
Chain (rear)	$\frac{1}{2}$in x .335in 120 pitches		Speedometer	80 mph

Engine and frame numbers

To the end of 1968, BSA used one system of numbering for both engines and frames. A year letter or two was followed by the model type and then the number. However engines and frames seldom matched, and sometimes the prefixes differed. To find the year of either engine or frame, you need the whole of the number, with all prefixes and suffixes. "S" in the frame prefix was often for rear suspension, "C" for competition, and "B" for battery lighting. The 1969 and later data is provided at the end.

Range	Year	Model	Engine	Rigid frame	Spring frame
D1	1949	D1 engine	UYD-101		
		D1	YD-101	YD1-101	
	1950	D1 engine	UYD-20001(Wico)		
		D1 engine	UYDL-101(Lucas)		
		D1	YD-20001	YD1-20001	YD1S-20001
		D1(Lucas)	YDL-101	YD1-20001	YD1S-20001
	1951	D1	YD1-40001	YD1-40001	YD1S-40001
		D1(Lucas)	YDL1-3001	YD1-40001	YD1S-40001
	1952	D1	YD1-63001	YD1-64001	YD1S-64001
		D1(Lucas)	YDL1-8001	YD1-64001	YD1S-64001
	1953	D1	BD2-101	BD2-101	BD2S-101
		D1(Lucas)	BD2L-101	BD2-101	BD2S-101
	1954	D1 direct	BD-101	BD2-14600	BD2S-14600
		D1 battery	BDB-101	BD2-14600	BD2S-14600

Range	Year	Model		Engine	Rigid frame	Spring frame
		D1	comp	BD-101	BD2-14600	BD2S-14600
	1955	D1	direct	DD-101	BD2-34701	BD2S-34701
		D1	battery	DDB-101	BD2-34701	BD2S-34701
		D1	comp	DD-101	BD2-34701	
D3	1954	D3	direct	BD3-101	BD2-14600	BD2S-14600
		D3	battery	BD3B-101	BD2-14600	BD2S-14600
		D3	comp	BD3-101	BD2-14600	BD2S-14600
	1955	D3	direct	BD3-5138	BD2-34701	BD2S-34701
		D3	battery	BD3B-5138	BD2-34701	BD2S-34701
		D3	comp	BD3-5138	BD2-34701	

Range	Year	Model	Engine Direct lights	Battery	Frame
D1	1956	D1	DD-4801	DDB-3301	BD2S-55001
	1957	D1	DD-	DDB-	BD2S-
	1958	D1	DD-8577	DDB-7849	BD2S-65001
	1959	D1	DD-10812	DDB-10628	BD2S-67581
	1960	D1	DD-12501	DDB-12501	BD2S-70501
	1961	D1	DD-14501	DDB-14501	BD2S-73701
	1962	D1	DD-15481	DDB-16413	BD2S-76680
	1963	D1	DD-16129	DDB-17606	BD2S-78746
D3	1956	D3	BD3-10401	BD3B-12801	CD3-101
	1957	D3	BD3-	BD3B-	CD3-
D5	1958	D5	ED5-101	ED5B-101	FD5-101
D7	1959	D7	ED7-101	ED7B-101	D7-101
	1960	D7	ED7-1501	ED7B-7001	D7-8101
	1961	D7	ED7-3001	ED7B-15501	D7-18401
	1962	D7	ED7-4501	ED7B-23001	D7-27450
	1963	D7	ED7-5505	ED7B-26904	D7-33268
		D7 Police		ED7BP-26904	D7-33268
		D7A (USA)	ED7A-5505	ED7BA-26904	D7-33268
		D7 Trail	ED7-5505		D7-33268T
	1964	D7	ED7-6887	FD7-101	D7-38400
		D7(USA)	ED7A-6887	FD7A-101	D7-38400
		D7 Trail	ED7-6887		D7-38400
	1965	D7	ED7-9001	FD7-3001	D7-42878
		D7 Pastoral	ED7-9001		D7-42878
		Trail Bronc	ED7-9001		D7-42878
	1966	D7 de luxe	ED7-101	FD7-9076	D7-49855 to 51960 & GD7-101 to 8616
	1966	D7 Silver	ED7-101	FD7-10127	D7-51320 to 51960 & GD7-101 to 8616

Range	Year	Model	Engine	Frame
D10	1967	D10	D10-01	D10-101
		D10S	D10A-101	D10A-101
		D10B	D10A-101	BD10A-101
D14	1968	D13		
		Supreme	D13B-101 to 780	D13B-101
		D13 Sports	D13B-101 to 780	D13B-101S
		D13		
		Bushman	D13C-101 to 780	C13C-101B
		D14/4	D14B-781	D14B-781
		D14/4S	D14B-781	D14B-781S
		D14/4B	D14C-781	D14C-781B

For 1969 and onwards, a new coding system was adopted by BSA using a) a two-letter prefix for month and year; b) the model type code, and c) the number.

Month code:

A	January	D	April	H	July	N	October
B	February	E	May	J	August	P	November
C	March	G	June	K	September	X	December

Year code: C September 1968-July 1969
D August 1969-July 1970
E August 1970-July 1971

Thus BC00115 signifies February 1969.
Within those dates, the following numbers apply

Engine	Frame	
D14C11333	11333	September 1968 D14 Sports, D14B Bushman discontinued
BC 00115	00115	February 1969 D175 and D175 Bushman start
04204	04204	November 1969 D175 continues
04658	04658	January 1970, D175 continues

Some approximate modern colour equivalents
D1 mist green — Ford mist green, Mercedes green
GPO D1 — Ault and Wiborg's GL11220 Post Office Red
(Polychromatic blue and red were created by a complicated process involving spraying over a base of silver. Bri-tie say they can reproduce this, but a full respray is not cheap).

Bantam: Useful Information
Books
BSA Gold Star and other Singles by Roy Bacon (Osprey)
BSA Singles Restoration by Roy Bacon (Osprey)

The Book of the BSA Bantam by W.C. Haycraft (Pitmans, o/p)
BSA Single Cylinder Motor Cycles by D. W. Munro (Pearsons, o/p)
BSA Bantam Superprofile by Jeff Clew (Foulis)
BSA Bantam Owners Workshop Manual by Jeff Clew (Haynes)

Bruce Main-Smith Ltd., PO Box 20, Leatherhead, Surrey (Tel: 0372 375616) A good selection of reprinted handbooks and parts lists.

Clubs

British Two Stroke Club: Membership secretary: Alan Abrahams, 38 Charles Drive, Cuxton, Rochester, Kent ME2 1DR. Eligible for VMCC insurance scheme.
BSA Owners Club: Membership secretary: Graham Howie, 11 Wallingford Avenue, Davyhulme, Manchester M31 1QN. Eligible for VMCC insurance scheme.
Bantam Racing Club: 6 Kipton Close, Rothwell, Northants. NN14 2DR.
Bantam Owners Club: Secretary: Mrs Peggy Clarke, 2 Willis Waye, King's Worthy, Winchester, Hants, SO23 7QT.

Shops

T and G, 4 The Parade, Wiltshire Road, Thornton Heath, Surrey (Tel: 01-684 1414).
Alan Shepherd, A and D Motorcycles, Spencer Industrial Estate, Denbigh, Clwyd (Tel: 074571 5105).
C and D Autos, 1193-1199 Warwick Road, Acocks Green, Birmingham B27 6BY (Tel 021-706 2901).
Bob Joyner, Wolverhampton Road, Warley, W. Midlands (Tel 021-552-2961).
MCS, 216 Leytonstone Road, London E11 (Tel 01-534 2711).
Bri-Tie Motorcycles, Cwnsannan, Llanfynydd, Carmarthen, Dyfed SA32 7TQ (Tel: 05584 579).

Chapter Nine

Villiers 9E Single and 2T Twin-engined machines

Villiers 9E and 2T machines: Background

Villiers riders are the insulted and injured of the old bike movement. Slow and not invariably reliable, the mass-produced 2-stroke engines from Wolverhampton powered lightweights for a dozen or more post-war marques, ranging from the respectable (Greeves) to the indifferent (James) to the diabolical (Tandon). 'Agricultural in concept, lacking any stamina, and decidedly fragile in design,' was how off-road man Don Morley put it, and he was far from alone in that opinion. Villiers represented the essence of utility biking, the ones for whom the term 'grey porridge' was coined, the ghetto you sought to break out of, into the sunlit uplands of 4-stroke parallel twin ownership.

Villiers never marketed complete machines, just the engine units. In their $17\frac{1}{2}$ acre site in Marston Road, Wolverhampton, everything, including exhaust systems and carburettors, was made in-house. Villiers engines also featured self-contained ignition, in the form of their flywheel magneto. This had been dreamed up at the onset of the First World War, when the supply of German magnetos dried up; the first prototype had been tested between two ladies' hatpins and two corks. The engineer responsible, Frank Farrer, became Chairman of the company from 1946 on, and a combination of this fact and a lack of much domestic competition in the lightweight field led to the effective stagnation of the design.

The same basic engine format served many, many uses in addition to motorcycles — chainsaws, rickshaws (from Dot), lawnmowers, industrial engines and generator sets, invalid carriages, three-wheelers (Bond etc), ultra-lightweight autocycles and even miniature railways — there's an 11E-engined train running to this day in Weston-Super-Mare. Production was on a grand scale with the overall 2 million engine mark reached in 1956 and the millionth motorcycle engine produced by 1960. The aim was not performance but a standard engine, precision built for reliability in the hands of Mr. Average. After take-over in 1965 as Norton-Villiers and subsequent collapse, the industrial engine side was revived by David Sankey and survives today, but the connection with motorcycles is nil.

In fact Villiers, among the alphabet soup of model numbers and letter categories for capacities (150cc C, 250cc single A, etc.) did produce some sturdy and usable roadster motors, and their dismissal by most enthusiasts means that prices today can be very cheap indeed. All you need to remember, in our opinion, is the 197cc single E, and 250 and 350 twin series. Narrowing it down further, only in fact models powered by the 9E/10E single which was produced from 1955 to 1966, plus the 2T 250 (1957-63), 350 3T (1958-63) and at a pinch the 4T (1963-66).

Concentrating on the 9E among all the singles may seem a little arbitrary, and it is true that it certainly makes life easier for the writer and probably the reader too! If information on the whole bewildering range of Villiers machinery, as well as other British 2-strokes, is required, the tireless Roy Bacon has come up with the goods in *Villiers Singles and Twins* in the Osprey Collectors' Library. His book is also the source for engine and frame numbers, where available, which space does not permit including here. But the 9E represents the true practical Villiers single today, and the twins are even more rideable and wonderfully smooth alternatives. Both were produced at a time when Villiers, by then beginning to lose out to competition on the mass markets, were practising a "segment retreat", i.e. making higher quality engines in smaller numbers. For the motorcycles they powered, the crudities of rigid and plunger rear ends were a thing of the past; all the roadsters that fitted them handled adequately, and some exceptionally well (Cotton, Greeves, etc.). Also, being born at the end of the era of all-purpose sports mounts, many of them possessed some of their competition relatives' good points, like a narrow turning circle and steering geometry which gives good low speed control. The ample mudguarding and panelling that bumped up their weight were at least built to last and have often done so, though missing tinware is usually the bane of restoring one of them.

All post-war Villiers roadster engines, with one exception, conformed to a similar pattern, with iron barrels, alloy heads, vertically-split aluminium alloy crankcases containing built-up crankshafts, with the transmission on the left and the flywheel magneto, in various forms, on the right; bolted to the rear of the engine in semi-unit form was the gearbox, with internals from Albion. (The exception was the first 125, which was of true unit construction.) The 9E, however, in response to the success of the Bantam, inclined its cylinder forward and reduced the size of its flywheel magneto to do away with the traditional saucepan-lid cover on the right side. It enclosed the gearbox end cover and kickstart mechanism, and thus produced a look called 'air-smoothed' to match the Bantam's egg-shaped cases. This had the effect of better, though not perfect, protection for the electrics, and within the covers the smaller flywheel meant remote mounting of the ignition coil, which in turn meant that larger ones could be fitted and the ignition improved. The crankshaft itself was thickened and the size of the double ball main bearings enlarged. Though claimed output for the roadsters was unchanged from the 8E's 8.4bhp at 4000rpm, the 9E was **75** the stronger engine, and provided top speeds in the mid-50s. The 9E proved a favourite with the off-road sportsman, with some companies (Dot, and eventually Greeves) turning over all their production to trials and scrambles machinery. The larger enclosed area within the crankcase cover, incidentally, allowed a larger, lead-weighted flywheel giving greater low-speed plonk to be fitted for the trials engines only, which are distinguished by a T-suffix. The competition popularity, now revived for pre-'65 events, means that spares for all versions of the 9E today are good, and helps explain why DMW, one firm surviving from that era, occasionally make up new engine spares, in addition to the large stock they took over from Villiers when the latter ceased production.

The first of the air-smoothed engines had been the 225cc 1H in 1953, but only a few roadsters featured this briefly (DMW Cortina, and some Francis-Barnetts and James), and top end spares for them today are difficult. In response to the demands of competition, there followed the 250 A series from 1958 on, but in road use this engine proved itself harsh, and again some spares are harder to come by than those for the ubiquitous 9E. The latter, featuring in roadsters from twelve marques, is the one for us.

Nevertheless, the 9E-engined roadsters are confined in several instances to a few specific years. In some cases, this is because companies ended all their production at the beginning of the 60s (Excelsior, Sun, Norman), or concentrated on other models (Dot, Panther). But in the case of the two biggest manufacturers, Francis-Barnett and James, it was because they kept on with the old 8E engine until 1957 and 1958 respectively when Villiers could oblige their parent Plumstead-based AMC company by producing a 10E version of the engine, identical to the 9E except for the upright cylinder

Nice enough body - shame about the engine. A Francis-Barnett Falcon 87 with the sunburst cylinder head finning which betrays that it's '59-on, powered by the 198cc AMC engine which the prudent avoid.

that AMC demanded for styling purposes.

Then for James in 1959 and Francis-Barnett in 1960 came AMC's own 2-stroke, a design they had commissioned from an Italian, Vincent Piatti. In four capacities from 150 to 250, these two-stroke singles featured an unusual piston crown, matched to a pair of deflectors cast into the cylinder head to project down into the bore. On these engines, all but the 150 being easily identifiable by 'sunburst' cylinder head finning, the piston to bore clearance thus became critical. Lacking experience in the precision work of 2-stroke assembly with its closer tolerances, building engines for James and Francis-Barnett at Plumstead, AMC rapidly got into difficulties.

It really was a specialist area, something recognised even by Triumph, who turned the engine-building for their 2-stroke Tina scooter over to the BSA group's Bantam factory at Redditch. Even if they had got it right, the AMC engine had no advantage over the Villiers equivalent, and in competition its weight and wide crankcases positively disadvantaged it. 'Just a bad design with a queer shaped combustion chamber' was how AMC development engineer Wally Wyatt summed it up. It was a doubly sad failure because the engines were housed in some good-looking, substantial and reasonably good-handling cycle parts — and due to different mounting points, cannot readily be interchanged with Villiers equivalents, though people used to do it. This was in contrast to Villiers themselves, where all the 'air-smoothed' engines, including the twins, had identical mounting points and could be swapped with one another. Finally Plumstead had to eat humble pie and in 1961 turn over assembly of the engines to Villiers, the very concern from whom the new design had been intended to liberate them. The AMC 200s lingered on until the group went under in 1966, so with Francis-Barnetts and James in that category, our choice is limited to a couple of years.

The twin engines also featured in most of the same dozen motorcycle marques, though they had been developed by Villiers for use in bubble cars. Essentially they were a pair of 125 singles, a fact emphasised by the air gap between the cylinders; the dimensions of the latter were very close to those of the 122cc B series engines, of 50 x 62mm, the 2T being 50 x 63.5. The twin engines were rubber-mounted, and a well-fettled example of the 250 2T provides a very pleasant ride indeed, with a modest but sufficient output of 15bhp at 5500rpm and a top speed of around 70mph, reached by some brisk acceleration above a slight power-step, though the latter did not diminish low-speed tractability. The 325cc 3T versions, bored out to 57mm, were also intended for 3-wheelers, but in a few instances (Cotton, DMW, Greeves, Panther) some got into the road bikes, and had even more torque than the 250s.

The later 4T 250 was designed for use in the Bond 3-wheeler, and was modified to avoid overheating beneath a bonnet. (For this application and for use in scooters, some versions of the twins were in fact available with fan cooling attached to their electric start system, another option, and there were also versions of both twin and single — the latter the 9E/4SFR variant — with reverse gear, ones to watch out for!) The 4T, together with **77** its ported pistons and angled head-finning, had transfer passages increased in number from two to four, so that they could be shallower, letting more air pass between the cylinders. They also featured less effective centre seals, which were as crucial to crankcase compression as the single's fibre seals; trials ace Peter Hammond at his shop used to substitute 2T seals in his customers' 4T engined roadsters. In addition, on the motorcycle 4T

Villiers-engined roadsters can be restored to a very attractive standard, and get a lot of attention when they are - like this rare banana-yellow and pale blue Greeves 25DC Sports Twin.

engine the output had been raised to 17bhp at 6000rpm, principally by higher 8.75:1 compression and the use of an exhaust system with tuned resonances. (Villiers then supplied the exhausts and silencers for their engines). The result, however, was a distinct loss of the 2T's strong bottom end torque, and a revvier, peakier engine. Riders preferred the 2T, but it was the later 4T that they usually got for 1964-1966, except in the case of firms like Cotton and Panther, who had stockpiled 2Ts. The same preference is wise today.

As mentioned, an electric start was an option on the 2T, the German Siba Dynastart which combined the dynamo and starter by having coils and brushes for both purposes, plus a suitable control box. In practical terms 12 volt batteries necessary for the system restricted underseat storage. The Dynastart works well, but only if its brushes are cleaned every 5-8000 miles, a chore that means removing the engine cover, ignition cam and

Something about the mundane Villiers engine often encouraged manufacturers to be fantastical, as with this 10E-engined James Captain in 1958.

rotor, which in turn requires a special rotor extractor tool. Engines so equipped have an S in the engine number. Their compression was raised to 10:1 to compensate for the generator's additional drag. An external clue 79 to their presence is that they lacked the 2T's cover over their carb. Though it worked well when it did, probably the Dynastart's complexities are best avoided, being one more thing to go wrong.

Good Villiers points are a strong enough, if clonky, gearbox and clutch, excellent spares interchangeability, and simplicity of maintenance. The single's understressed nature makes it a viable if unexciting day-in, day-out ride, while some of the twins are probably the best all-rounders among the lightweights which this book recommends, even if at from 260-300lb dry, they are pushing the outside of the ''lightweight'' envelope. As with the Bantams, the fact that so many people actually rode a James or Francis-Barnett, even if they were yearning for a Triumph, means that while riding one you tap a rich vein of nostalgia in the older generation, and well-restored Villiers-engined bikes always get a lot of attention at shows and the like. Some of these lightweights' styling is flamboyant to the point of fantasy (Ambassador, Greeves 25DCX), while some embodied genuinely attractive Italian-type sports style (Cotton Vulcan Sport, James' Superswift, etc.). And there's a strong camaraderie among Villiers 2-stroke riders, wilfully unfashionable individuals even in the British biking sub-culture, a league of the insulted and injured.

Villiers 9E and 2T engines, and the machines they powered

Here is a brief technical description of both the 9E single and 2T twin engine, followed by a necessarily quick look at the various marques and models which they graced with their presence.

The 9E followed the general layout of previous Villiers singles with their vertically split crankcases, but differed from them in dropping the previous big flywheel on the right with its saucepan lid-type circular cover, and featuring a smaller flywheel magneto behind a streamlined oval-shaped right-hand crankcase cover. This was embellished with styling strips, and featured a detachable plate for access to the flywheel mag; this plate, and for the twins a matching one on the left-side cover, usually bore the Villiers name, but sometimes that of the end user motorcycle firm, or occasionally one on either side. The new right-hand cover also contained the kickstart mechanism and the gearbox casing, so there was a hole in it for clutch adjustment. The built-up crankshaft was slightly stronger than previously, and ran on a single ball race on the timing side, with on the drive side two ball race bearings of different diameters, so that there was a step in the crankshaft to accommodate them. Don Morley identifies this as a potential fracture point in competition, especially scrambles, machinery. Villiers' two-stroke expert Nick Kelly confirms that this was never a problem with the less-stressed roadsters, however, though a roller-bearing conversion favoured by the competition folk can be adopted by the ultra-cautious.

The 9E engine, with its cylinder inclined 10° forward, featured an alloy head with a hemispherical combustion chamber and the sparking plug set in the right-hand side at an angle. The iron barrel was held down by four

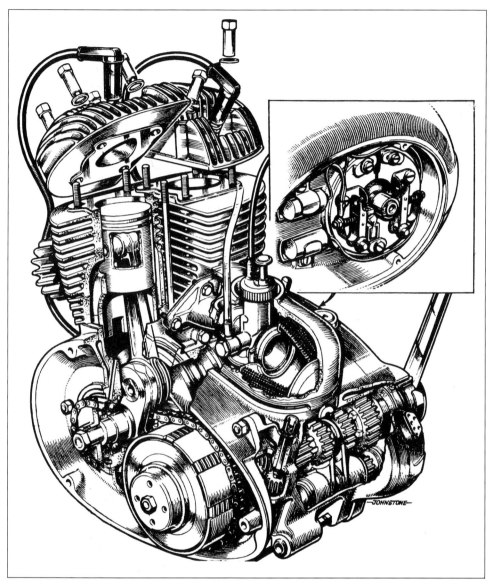

Villiers 2T engine anatomized.

studs, the exhaust port at the front was low on the left-hand side, and at the rear there was an inlet stub for a single Villiers S25 carburettor with concentric float chamber and integral air cleaner. The characteristically long and heavy Villiers flat-topped alloy piston ran on a steel conrod with a bronze bush small end and uncaged double-row roller big end bearings, between twin half-circle crankweb bobweights. The porting arrangement was of the simple Villiers post-war type with one inlet, one exhaust and two transfer ports.

The 9E was part of the Villiers 'air-smoothed' range of singles, all broadly similar.

Primary transmission was by a single-row chain, and its tension was determined by the number of paper gaskets between the engine and gearbox, which ranged from one to four; if more were needed, it was time to renew the chain. The wet clutch was a 9-spring, 3-plate design; there was a 2-spring version of it, but the 9-spring was the one for motorcycle use. The gearbox, though it gave the appearance of unit-construction, was in fact semi-unit, being bolted up to the rear of the flywheel magneto's case, with the assembly hollowed out on top to clear the carburettor float chamber. The Albion internals were as substantial and as clonky as that firm's similar production for Royal Enfield, and for the 9E were a complete redesign on the previous models, with new internal gear sizes and profiles. This meant that, unusually for a Villiers, they were not interchangeable with their predecessors, though they were in common with their A-series 250 successors. The box came with wide or standard ratios, in 3- or 4-speed versions, the latter being most common. There was no external gear-position indicator, so it is always worth checking which type is featured in a particular machine. There were minor internal modifications to the gearbox from 1961 on.

The 6 volt electrics were by a new, smaller version of the familiar flywheel magneto, with six poles and a remote outboard ignition cam. The flywheel itself was located on the crankshaft by a key and locked on a taper by a single centre nut, which also served as an extractor. The points and condenser were accessible inside the detachable cover plate, with the ignition coils remotely mounted. The HT spark plug pick-up ran from the magneto via a Bakelite moulding screwed into the front of the casing at an angle, and containing a simple spring and pad which made contact with the magneto's internal HT coil. A key-operated ignition switch was set in the upper surface of the cover.

The 9E unit weighed 64lb all up, and its mounting points were in common with the other 'air-smoothed' engines, i.e. the 148cc 31C, the 173cc 3L, the 197cc 11E, the 224cc 1H, the 246cc 2H and 31A-37A, and the 2T, 3T and 4T twins. This can be useful, as there are many engines about,

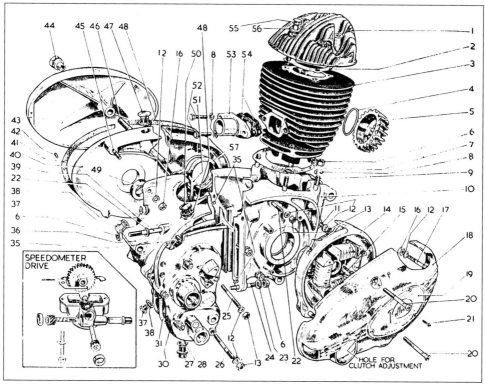

Exploded 9E inset shows speedometer drive assembly.

which can be transplanted into what is today much rarer, a bike with intact and decent cycle parts.

The 2T twin resembled the 9E singles in many ways. The separate barrels were iron, and inclined forward at a slight angle. The twin alloy heads with rearward facing sparking plugs featured a hemispherical pear shape combustion chamber, and the full skirt, two-ring, flat-top pistons were of alloy. The big ends had roller bearings. Compression ratio was 8.2:1, rising to 8.7 or 9.4:1 on the Sports and 10:1 on the Super Sports or Dynastart versions. Primary drive was by single chain to the wet four-plate clutch, and the 4-speed gearbox was bolted to the rear of the engine, with chain adjustment by paper gaskets. Standard or wide ratios were available. With the twin an external gear indicator was fitted. A single Villiers S22/2 carburettor was fitted, enclosed beneath a cover, with a plunger-operated air slide.

Within the rubber-mounted crankcases was a 180° crank, and both these features made for a notably smooth engine. The built-up, pressed-together crankshaft also ran on three bearings, but for the twin these comprised a ball bearing on the drive side, and roller bearings in the centre and on the right. The middle bearing, housed in a circular centre plate, meant that the cases had to be split if the seals were to be renewed, but it kept **83** engine width down to that of the single. Main bearing lubrication was assisted by oil drain holes in the crankcase.

Ignition was by flywheel magneto which, like the singles, had a remote outboard single-lobe cam keyed to an extension of the mainshaft, and supplied low tension current to separate contact breakers for each cylinder. These contact breakers were energised, via one of the two condensers on the armature plate, by a separate ignition circuit for each cylinder. This meant that with the help of a dial gauge, each cylinder could be timed independently, a highly desirable state of affairs which four-stroke twins like BSA and Triumph only attained in the mid-60s.

The 2T weighed 94lb, or 114lb if the Dynastart was fitted.

Now for an alphabetical review of the models into which these powerplants were fitted. Further details of them can be found in Roy Bacon's *Villiers Two-Stroke Singles and Twins*, and for the twins, in my own *British Motor Cycles since 1950* series. It should be noted that these mostly modest concerns, scattered up and down the country, would normally use the same basic frame layout for both singles and twins (though sometimes with different engine plates), something the common mounting points of the engines encouraged. So once again swaps and transplants between different models can be carried out. The same goes for many of the components which were common between most of the marques - British Hub Company wheels, for instance, Armstrong or Girling rear units, Burgess silencers, Metal Profile forks, or the Speedwell kidney-shaped sports tank found on the sportsters from Cotton, Norman, James, etc. This makes autojumbling for Villiers-engined bikes potentially fruitful.

Ambassador

Based in Ascot and run by Kaye Don, an ex-record breaker, Ambassador were unusual in not offering competition machinery. But their roadsters were built to a high standard and their single loop welded swinging-arm frames of the late 50s handled excellently. In addition, they incorporated some delightfully extravagant fairground styling, courtesy of ex-Norton man, Edgar Franks.

The 9E single models commenced with the Envoy, made from 1955 to 1959, with a 4-speed box as standard, but the 3-speed optional. This was followed by the 1959 3-Star Special, an Alex Frick design, with an Indian-style front mudguard and shapely enough partial rear enclosure. Finished in black and white, and a heavy example of the lightweight single breed at around 250lb dry, the 3-Star Special nevertheless handled well, despite its undamped front forks, with good adjustable Girlings at the rear, and reasonable 6in brakes at each end. It was supplemented for 1962 alone by the cut-price 9E-engined Popular, probably to clear stocks of the 3-speed version of the engine which was fitted. Not all the design touches were happy — the handlebar-cowling obscured part of the speedometer, and the oil measuring cup was attached to the filler cap inside the tank by

a lavatory-type chain. The machine gave a comfortable ride, with the 9E's usual 45mph cruising and 55mph top speed.

The 2T engined models began with the maroon and black Supreme Twin for 1957-1958, with conventional styling. This gave way for 1959-63 to the flamboyant Super S with similar front mudguard and panelling to the 3 Star Special, as well as a new front fork, wheels fashionably down from 18 to 17in, and good, if spongy, 7in brakes. Handling of these later twins was markedly superior. 1961-64 brought a new all-welded pivoted rear fork, and the black and gold 12-volt electric-start version, the Electra 75.

The Ambassador Super S twin was a revelation to the author.

For 1962-63 there was the Sports Twin, a sports-style version of the Super S, but in 1962 Kaye Don sold up the motorcycle side to DMW, so from '63 to '65 all models featured DMW wheels, hubs, brakes, and from mid-'63, a main frame loop in DMW-style squared tubing, new front forks and the enclosure in fibreglass rather than the previous pressed steel; the twins were virtually DMW IIMs with a different tank and round section swinging-arms. The Ambassadors did not survive the shift to the 4T engine in 1964, with the Electra 75 the last to be offered in 1965.

Good-looking and distinctive, it was a test ride on an Electra 75 which made me fully aware of how good a well-assembled 2T-engined machine could be. Prices today can be around £150-£200 for a single on the road, and £200-£350 for a running twin, though complete ones in good order can fetch up to £600.

Cotton

A firm with a distinctly sporting slant, the Cotton roadsters benefited from this with their low-set, loop-type, all-welded frame, and from the mid-50s

Cotton's tuned Continental Sports was a good-looking light twin.

were among the very best-handling Villiers-powered lightweights. The little Gloucester-based firm were innovative engineers, as evidenced by their own 1961 design of rear cush hub, which was manufactured for them by DMW/Metal Profiles and used by almost every other remaining lightweight manufacturer.

9E-engined Cotton roadsters began from 1955 to 1963 with the Vulcan, which was available in either three or four speeds, and from 1956 was slotted into their new swinging-arm frame. In 1958 this gained Armstrong leading-link forks, and in 1959 followed the trend to rear enclosure. In 1961 to 1968 came the red and black Vulcan Sports, with reduced rear enclosure, ace bars, flyscreen and slim mudguards; the standard Vulcan could have the abbreviated panelling then too, till its end two years later.

2T-engined Cottons began in 1957 with the Herald, and in 1958 like the singles these were fitted with an Armstrong leading-link fork. Already tested on the competition models, the new fork was concealed behind pressed steel shrouds accompanying an ugly mudguard mounted at a silly angle. This did not detract from the fork's performance, with all tests from then on agreeing that it provided hairline steering. Cotton's styling and detail finish remained their weak point, however, as evidenced by the dubious looks of the 1959 3T-engined Messenger with, as an option, possibly the ugliest full rear enclosure seen on any British model. It was compensated for by brakes up from 6 to 7in, good comfort, and the excellent suspension and handling of its single-downtube frame. Both it and the Herald were **86** offered alternatively with truncated panelling, and from 1961 came a pair of sports twins.

The Double Gloucester featured the same engine and frame, with that year's modification, Silentbloc bushes in the rear pivot, but front forks based on those used on Cotton's scrambler, rear panelling further reduced, and dropped bars, flyscreen and narrow mudguards as on the Vulcan Sports single. The two-tone Continental Sports featured both a new duplex downtube frame, Italian wheels with larger brakes, the new cush-drive at the rear, and a tuned engine which returned 78mph on one test. From 1963-67 it was joined by the Continental De Luxe, with mudguards valanced but still narrow and chromed, and British Hub wheels. In 1964 all twins adopted the duplex frame, and 1965 saw just the Herald and Continental extant, and fitted as standard with the harsh 4T until the end, though the 2T continued to be offered as an option until out of stock.

One problem with some 4-speed models was overgearing due to a 52-tooth rear wheel sprocket, which made them virtually 3-speeders with an overdrive. But the Cotton's excellent handling, in Nick Kelly's opinion better than the Greeves, makes it one for the hard rider to seek out. Prices will be similar to those of the Ambassador.

DMW

With Greeves, the exclusive DMWs are probably the most desirable of the Villiers-engined lightweights. With the company run by enthusiast Harold Nock and the machines built up to a standard, they were about the most expensive British two-stroke roadsters available. The DMW works also supplied hubs and brakes for most of the other lightweights, their own brakes from 1959 featuring a method of tappet-action shoe expansion developed from a Girling patent. The works also housed the Metal Profile company who built both telescopic and bottom link forks for several other marques. DMW's own special feature was the use of Talbot square-section tubing for their strong, versatile and good-handling frame. It was lugless, with sets of pressings forming the engine plates, fork pivot and panelling, and thus readily adaptable to different engine sizes.

A 9E-engined DMW roadster built from 1956 to 1965 was the four-speed 200P Mk 9. It was housed in a version of the square-section frame with its oval-section pivoted rear fork. Designed by ex-BSA man Mike Riley, with the ISDT principally in mind, these were light, tough, all-welded chassis. At the front went Metal Profiles' own bottom link front fork carrying their own hubs, all as supplied to Dot, Sun, etc. The tapered valanced front mudguard, and the way the pressings formed a rear mudguard and enclosure for the battery, the toolbox, and the mounting for the distinctive DMW wavy-topped dual seat, all made for a solid yet shapely look very reminiscent of contemporary continental, and specifically German DKW styling. One special Riley-designed feature was snail-cam adjustment for the rear chain, so that tension was identical on both sides; BSA singles didn't get this until 1971!

Handsomely finished in characteristic maroon-lined Paris Grey, blue, **87** or black, with a maroon seat for the grey option and a black one for the rest, the 200P Mk 9 featured the bottom link fork as an option, 3.25 x 18in tyres and wheels and 6in brakes in full width hubs front and rear, the latter being q.d. It continued with few changes, just a 1957 maroon and gold colour option, and the new hubs and S-type brakes for 1960. As part of the alternative M-framed series for 1963, there were detail changes which are described below for the twins. At the end of that year the previous P-series 9E machine went, followed at the end of 1965 by the M-series one. A quality option, these singles were, however, on the heavy side at 244lb.

2T-engined DMWs are one of the top options, beginning with the 1957-1966 Dolomite II. The Dolomite was styled and P-framed much as the single, with the bottom link fork also optional. Like the single, it got new and very effective brakes for 1960. In 1961 the 3T-engined Dolomite IIA was offered, and 1962 saw the merging with Ambassador, and hence the 1963 Dolomite IIM featuring straight-tube Earles forks where appropriate, and when fitted with telescopic forks, a new Ambassador-type front fork, with hydraulic damping as well as cast light-alloy sliders off DMW's own Hornet racer. A $3\frac{1}{4}$ gallon kidney-shaped tank, new headlamp shell for the 7in headlamp, an unusually loud horn, the extensive use of Nyloc nuts, the plastic bellows on the cable ends, and the 3-position Girling dampers, were all further examples of DMW's attention to detail.

1964 brought the inevitable shifts to the 4T for both the Dolomite II and Dolomite Sports, a 1963-1964 alternative was low handlebars, alloy mudguards and an Italian Red gold-lined petrol tank. 1965 brought back the previous K-frame and the plain but 4T-engined Dolomite II again. Both models ended in 1966.

If you are lucky enough to find a DMW, especially the twin, you will have a good-looking, good-handling machine — and one that the DMW works, still in existence producing and supplying Villiers spares as well as overhauling and servicing engines, will frankly favour above other marques! Prices are similar to the Ambassador or even a little higher.

Dot

The Manchester-based company, under Burnard Scott-Wade, were in the front-line of 2-stroke competition, and eventually turned their whole production over to that side. But they did briefly produce a solidly engineered 9E roadster model. This was the 1956-58 4-speed Mancunian, with competition-derived steel single-loop frame and Metal Profiles leading link front forks controlled by Armstrong units, housing a 19in wheel with a double-sided 6in front brake. The swinging-arm rear had Girling units and a 19in wheel with a single 6in brake. For 1958 a 3-speeder was an option, before the model was dropped. Likely to be well-built, these rare roadsters will probably turn up only close to their point of origin. An owners club indicates enthusiasm for the marque and its sporting achievements. The roadster's price would be low.

DMW Dolomite II, one of the best of British lightweights, but from 1964 powered by the harsher 4T engine, like this 1965 example.

Excelsior

A firm better known for pre-war racers, in wartime for the folding 98cc Welbike and post-war for their own not very exciting 2-stroke engined twins, for a few years Excelsior also produced 9E roadsters. The first was the haughtily-named 1956-57 4-speed A9 Autocrat in a single loop swinging-arm frame with their own brand telescopic forks, finished in black with a dualseat and rectified lighting. Then there was a gap until the 4-speed 10E-engined R10 from 1959-60, and the 1960-61 R11. Staid, bread-and-butter machines of no distinction bar a low weight of just over 200lb and a reputation for respectable handling. Nobody values these, so a low, low price.

Francis-Barnett

Francis-Barnett was one of the two volume lightweight producers, the other being James, and in this post-war period the Coventry firm with the funny name was the better of the two in many respects. But our area of interest is restricted, as already recounted, by the intervention of the beastly AMC engine.

There were a bewildering number of Francis-Barnett names and numbers, but 'Falcon' is the one to concentrate on for the 197cc singles. The 10E-engined Fanny-Bs were just the 1958-59 Falcon 81 models, and very handsome they were too, with clean-cut lines justifying the insistence on an upright engine, and emphasised by all-over Arden Green set off by gold lining and circular red, white and gold tank badges. The Falcon range's slim single-downtube front frame, with telescopics inherited from 89

James plus good adjustable Girling units at the rear, offered fair handling, and the simple styling was very pleasing, in particular the clean fork top area and mounting for the 6in headlamp, the long rounded-off side-covers concealing the rear frame, the rounded AMC-style mudguards and the way the shapely 2¾ gallon petrol tank blended with the short wraparound dark green dualseat. With 3.25 x 18in wheels front and rear, and full width hubs for the 5in brakes, a trim 49½in wheelbase and a weight of 244lb, this was an unassuming, compact general purpose lightweight. Then came the 1960 Falcon 87 with the AMC 200 engine. It's worth noting that its cycle parts were near-identical with the 9E-engined 81, so creative cannibalisation or a hybrid might be possible.

For the 2T-engined Francis-Barnetts, the key word is Cruiser. With that title at first appropriated by machines with the 224cc Villiers 1H, and then by those with the AMC 250 engine, the first 2T-engined machine was the Cruiser 89 which ran from 1962 until 1966. The Cruisers' frames had always been distinctive, and parts of it plus its forks had featured (with unhappy results) on Norton's Jubilee 250 twin. For the F-B twin, its basis was an oval, L-shaped, tapered down tube, formed from a single pressing and then bronze-welded to the malleable steering head lug. To this beam were bolted twin tubular loops forming the engine cradle, rear sub-frame and top tubes; in place of the seat tube there was a fabricated pressed-steel box member, with a structure welded to it forming both the rear mount for the engine and the swinging-arm spindle housing. At the front there were forks that also went on the Jubilee and on AMC's 'light-weight' AJS /Matchless 250 four-stroke singles, and at the rear 3-position Girlings. The combination, for the 313lb Cruisers at least, gave a hardish but respectable ride, with handling not at all bad. Tyres and wheels were 3.25 x 18in, and in full-width hubs the brakes were 6in front and rear, the latter at least rod-operated and effective enough, where the former was not.

All this was as for the AMC-engined preceding Cruiser 80; there had also been a very fully panelled AMC-engined version, the Leader-like Cruiser 84. The Cruiser 89 escaped these excesses, but as well as the sober all-Arden Green finish, it was offered in two-tone options of Arden Green for the front and for the petrol tank upper, and white for the lower tank, the side panels and the rear mudguard, or the same arrangement in black and white. Unhappily changing to the 4T engine for 1964 on, with only minor changes, the Cruiser 89 ran till the company's end in 1966.

It was, however, accompanied from 1963 to 1966 by the Sports Cruiser 91, and this was not just a Sports-styled 89. In 1962, due to AMC's troubles, Francis-Barnett had been forced to move in with James in Greet, Birmingham, and some subsequent badge-engineering went against the folk from Coventry. The Sports Cruiser 91 is in fact the Italian-look James Sports Superswift, which was nice-looking with the regulation sports bars, flyscreen, two-tone green and white finish, polished alloy guards, 2.75 x 19in front wheel, rearset footrests and gear-change plus a pretty 2¾ gallon kidney-shaped tank. But the James' tubular frames' handling was not good at all. It also swapped to the 4T engine for 1964.

Francis-Barnett's Cruiser 89, solidly built, substituted the reliable 2T for the dodgy AMC 250 single in 1962.

Either the Falcon 81 or the pre-'64 Cruiser 89 would make nice, solid, well-finished lightweights, with prices around the £200-£300 mark for the twins and around £50 less for the single. With so many built and so much of the tinware interchangeable, you are more likely than with almost any of the other marques to get lucky looking for cycle parts in job lots or at autojumbles; and Autocycle do hold some cycle parts spares. But can you live with a machine they called Fanny?

Greeves

Greeves are the recognised guvnors on the Villiers 2-stroke scene. Run in Essex by enthusiast Bert Greeves and his paraplegic cousin Derry Preston-Cobb, the motorcycle side was funded by production of Invacar invalid carriages. Greeves were distinguished by innovative suspension systems developed from those used on the Invacar, by quality build, and after the 1958 arrival of brilliant rider and development engineer Brian Stonebridge, for progressively transforming the staid Villiers single engine basic item into high performance competition motors which they eventually produced entirely themselves, the process not stopping with Stonebridge's untimely death in a 1960 road accident. They were undisputed leaders in the trials and scrambles field, with road race successes following, and this sports glamour has invested all their products with a desirable aura. If they fell down in any area, it was just with the gawky looks of the earlier machines, and perhaps the earlier suspension systems. This popularity was the same when the machines, including the roadsters, were new, with the limited output, possible because the firm did not rely on motorcycle sales, being snapped up in advance by enthusiastic buyers. Expensive then, the same applies now, and most Greeves will be beyond our price range. But the odd roadster may come up for a reasonable sum.

The 9E-engined Greeves began in 1956 to 1958 with the 20D Fleetstar models, which were all 4-speed. They were housed, with just different engine plates and several spacers, in the same unique alloy beam frame as the company's twins, which at that stage, like most other companies' two-stroke twins, were British Anzani-engined. One criticism was that the spacers were not, as was the case with Norman, welded on to the engine plates, which made fitting an engine somewhat fiddly. Quality Greeves touches for that year included a new light blue dualseat and beneath its rear, a detachable toolbox. But the big attraction was the rigid and strong beam frame which contributed so much to the good handling, and the rubber-in-torsion pivoted fork front suspension, a palpably good performer which even if it would become outclassed in competition, was more than adequate on the road; although these early versions juddered under heavy braking.

So the Greeves' taut handling was a very strong suit, and the machines were also noted for their smoothness. The rear end had been rubber-in-torsion too, but both to counter sales resistance and because it had been less than perfect, a conventional swinging-arm set up with non-adjustable Armstrong hydraulic dampers had been adopted, though the swinging-arm still relied on Metalastic rubber and metal bushes which formed part of the rear fork pivot. The 20D had the twins' big $3\frac{5}{8}$ gallon tank, with as a badge, a handsome and distinctive alloy plate bearing a facsimile of Bert Greeves' signature. With detail changes, its looks, with the Moorland Blue and grey finish, were an improvement on the previous year's offerings, despite the ungainly front mudguard which the forks dictated.

There were only detail changes for the 20D for 1957 and 1958, and the roadster 197 was dropped in 1959 in favour of a 31A-engined 246cc single in a redesigned frame, but the A-series engine was rather lumpy where the 9E was smooth. The 9E in roadster form didn't make its reappearance until 1961-1966 with the 20DB, soon 20DC, Sports single. This now enjoyed the other model's improved '57-on front forks with Girling units replacing the previous adjustable friction damper, though with torsion rubbers still controlling the damping, as well as a beam frame modified in line with the top-selling 20TA Scottish Trials bike with a 2% steeper steering head angle, a 20% improvement in lock, and a slightly shorter
wheelbase. The four-speed engine had that year's Villiers gearbox

Hard competition like this 1963 SSDT forged the Greeves' strength and first class handling, making them the most popular British lightweight among sporting riders.

modification, and styling was tighter, with the angled nacelle headlamp and conventional slim polished alloy mudguards, and a dark blue tank with gold lining. Radial finned brake drums were an optional extra.

As other roadsters came and went, the 20DC carried on in this form, handsome, well-finished, and good handling; some found the leading-links fork an acquired taste, though it was no better or worse than any Armstrong-forked roadster. With fair 6in brakes and weight on the substantial side at 270lb dry, it remained until the end of roadster production, which had been increasingly overtaken by the concentration on competition, in 1966.

The 2T-engine models began in 1957 with a 25D Fleetwing, though that name and number had already featured with a British Anzani-engined 250 twin which lingered for the 2T machines' first year, so watch out not to confuse the two if buying. The new machine featured the beam frame and revised forks with dampers as on the single. Like the other roadsters, the 25D that year featured a new dualseat with its Vynide cover prominently finished in pale blue checks! But it also fitted a dual 6in brake on its 20in front wheel, welcome in view of its dry weight of around 260lb and a top speed just under 70mph. 'Retardation proved commendably smooth and rapid' said *Motor Cycling* tester, but a braking figure of 36ft from 30mph scarcely bore that out. Otherwise testers loved the handling and the lively twin engine, notably smooth up to 60mph.

Unchanged for 1958, the roadster was renamed the 25DB Sports Twin for 1959-60. In 1959 it underwent effective restyling of its cycle parts, with, as on the single, narrow polished alloy guards, a shapely tubular pressing for the 6in headlamp, and a peak for its chrome surround, a 2½ gallon tank and a rear wheel down from 20 to 19in. The front went from 20 to 19in with SLS single 6in brakes front and rear, a siamesed exhaust system with a Villiers silencer on the left, Moorland Blue and grey finish and a more restrained dualseat, with just light-coloured sides. Cycle parts in fact were identical with those of the 31A 246cc engined single, with the finned brakes an option.

For 1960-1963, this twin was joined in 1960 by a few examples only of the 3T-engined 32DB, with 8.7:1 compression ratio, 5mph more at the top end, plus improved torque. In 1961 the 250's compression was raised and its output went up to 17bhp, and more of the 3T-engined machines were produced, now as the 32DC, with the 250 now the 25DC. The fork was stiffened and the beam frame now used needle-roller bearings in an enlarged steering head, the rear fork arms were set wider apart to allow a wide off-road tyre, and a previous subsidiary frame discarded; this sub-frame had supported the seat, whose height was thus lowered an inch to 30½in.

From May 1962 to 1966 Greeves succumbed gloriously to a current fad for Italian-styled sports roadsters, with the 25DCX Sportsman Twin, weird

and wonderfully finished in pale blue and banana yellow, with even a red seat on some models. Greeves' own fibreglass was used for the kidney-shaped petrol tank and for a handlebar fairing with flyscreen and instrument console, as well as for the spats on the front forks. Full-width alloy hubs with an air scoop were fitted. For sobriety's sake, the 25DCX was accompanied for 1963 to 1965 by the new 25DD Essex

Bananarama. A bunch of nicely-finished yellow and blue 2T-engined Greeves 25DC Sports twins about to leave the factory.

Twin, which ran alongside the 25DC Sports Twin, and fitted valanced alloy mudguards, twin exhaust, a short flat handlebar and the DCX's tank but in a gold-lined all-Moorland Blue finish, plus for 1964 an alternative two-tone blue finish with black seat.

1964 saw the coming of the 4T, though the 2T could still be had for the 25DC Sports Twin, as could the 3T engine for older models. The unsuccessful 25DCX was now to special order only. 1965 brought just the 25DC Sports Twin, as well as a police version of the Essex, the 24DF, and the 25DC Mk II East Coaster, so named not for Essex but for the Eastern Seaboard of the United States, the country to which many Greeves were exported. But its 4T engine was prone to all that powerplant's troubles, including difficult starting. Both machines could feature full-width hubs, though for the DC they were optional extras. The 24DF Police version eventually endorsed the general opinion of the peaky 4T engine by swapping to heavier Siba-version flywheels and also fitting 2T barrels. 1966 was the last year for all, though 4T-engined twins and 35A-engined singles, both with Dynastarts, continued to be supplied to the Police until 1968.

The 2T-engined '59-'60 DB and '61-'64 Sports Twin were probably the best looking models. The problem remains money. Any Greeves now can fetch £350-£450, with good examples £200-£300 more, though with the singles it may be possible to come on one up to £100 cheaper. They were and are undoubtedly desirable machines, and by now too many people know it.

This 1964 Greeves Essex Twin shows beam frame and leading link forks (behind plastic spats) typical of the breed, but it was powered by the 4T.

James

Though a substantial name in the lightweight world, after the 1951 AMC takeover, the retirement of their long-time Managing Director, the **95** conscientious and accessible Fred Kimberley, and the departure of trials star and development man Bill Lomas in 1954, the James story was not a very happy one. Their 1955 swinging-arm frame for the singles, while very adequate for roadsters, for competition work had a reputation for weakness which undercut Lomas's earlier sensational Villiers-powered success. Then AMC, already having imposed some badge-engineering, and well aware of its own Piatti engine's deficiencies, cut competition involvement altogether for a while. Francis-Barnett moved in with them in 1962, and with both AMC and the market failing fast, the last James twins were equipped with another poor-handling chassis. These were not vintage years for the Greet, Birmingham company.

The 10E-engined James which the upright cylinder AMC had demanded was produced for one year only, as the 1958 K7 Captain. James' equivalent of Francis-Barnett's Arden Green was maroon, and the K7 Captain was optionally finished in this, with gold-lined grey tank panels and a grey seat, while the standard finish was dark grey with blue tank panels. The Captain was a smart machine with clean lines, and a respectable dry weight of 220lb. The swinging-arm frame and telescopic forks with minor variations were the same as the 8E-engined K7 and K12 Colonel since 1955, with well-valanced mudguards and 3 x 18in tyres and wheels bearing full-width hubs and indifferent 5in brakes front and rear; adjustable Girling units went at the rear. A solid model with acceptable road handling, the following year it was replaced by the AMC-engined L20 Captain.

The 2T-engined models began in 1962 with the M25 Superswift. The Villiers engine went in a frame already in use for the AMC-engined L25,

Trim 1958 James Captain 200, for years equipped with the upright 10E version of the Villiers 9E which AMC insisted on being specially made for their machines. Then they dropped it and tried building their own . . .

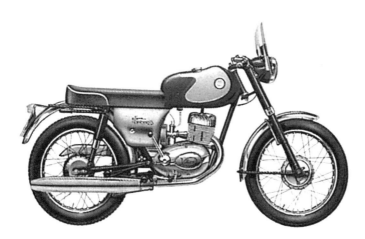

Sharply styled 1964 M25S James Sport Superswift, but flawed by the 4T engine and poor handling.

with a single top and downtube which bolted to a centre section and rear mudguard built up from pressings. One necessary change with the move to Villiers power was making the right-hand footrest hinged to accommodate the 2T's kickstart. This chassis provided decent handling, combined with the solid continental-style looks of many French and German machines of the period, of a Jawa or, closer to home, of the DMWs, though the latter did it better. Finished in blue and silver, with chrome tank panels, a couple of nicely integrated styling features on the Superswift were the shape of the piping on the seat, and a fully-enclosed rear chaincase built up around the swinging-arm, with a rear-pointing proboscis like a dolphin. The 6in brakes front and rear were not too good, with the rear brake pedal a two-piece fabrication, leading to flexing and a 35ft stopping distance from 30mph, but altogether the 300lb Superswift was a fair cruiser — especially when fitted with the optionally available whitewall tyres.

The same could not be said of the M25 Sports Superswift, which was offered in 1963. In it the M25's pressed steel rear end was supplanted by a tubular assembly, and the frame thus created provided notably poor handling. A pity, as with a mildly tuned engine, and flyscreen, dropped bars, polished alloy mudguards, rearset footrests and gear pedal and the kidney-shaped tank, this slim blue and silver Sports with its chrome battery and toolbox lids was a sharp looker. It, like the M25 Superswift, switched to the 4T engine from 1964 until the end.

As with Francis-Barnett, a lot of James were produced, so searching for cycle parts for one has a better hope of success than most. Prices too are around the Francis-Barnett level.

Norman

Built in Ashford, Kent, by brothers Fred and Charlie, Norman Cycles were known for good finish whether on bicycles, mopeds, or their innovatory competition machines — they were among the first in the field with swinging-arm rear suspension in 1952, in an unconventional cantilever frame **97**

1961 9E-engined Norman B2SDL, built in Kent.

from their own tube craftsmen. Their styling could be quaint, but by the end they had got it more or less right, as well as achieving excellent standards of handling, which they developed by road racing.

The 2T-engined Norman roadsters began in 1958 to 1960 with the B3 Twin. This featured a swinging-arm single downtube frame with separate engine plates, like a Greeves. At the front, with the Armstrong bottom link forks that Fred Norman had helped Armstrong develop for trials work, there was a big front mudguard; further back there were some excruciating wavy sheet steel sidepanels. The B3 was fairly heavy at 307lb, but already handled and steered well at speed, with the fairly upright forks and minimal trail giving good low speed handling too. A 3 x 19in front wheel was fitted, but in full-width hubs the 6in brakes were not good. 1959 brought a B3 Sports version, with the styling cleaned up and a red tank with knee recesses, dropped bars, alloy guards and flyscreen. A Norman was second in its class in the Thruxton 500 mile race that year.

1961-1962 brought the revised maroon and black B4 model, with a 14lb weight saving; steel plates still formed the engine cradle, but the rear sub-frame became a rigid triangulated structure replacing the single vertical

Sporty 1961 Norman B4 Sports.

seat tube. The leading link forks were revised, the fine handling kept intact, but the 6in brakes, though modified, were still not good. There was a spectacular Italian-type B4 Sports version in ruby red and ivory with a $3\frac{3}{4}$ gallon petrol tank of Tebaldi design, and a tuned 10:1 compression ratio engine. Everything stopped at the end of 1961 when Norman sold out to Raleigh Cycles.

If you can find one, these are good sporting machines, with the 1961-on models handling better due to the modified swinging-arm pivot. Prices should be around the Ambassador level, though without the high top price.

Panther

Normally associated with the slogging sloper sidecar-hauling 4-stroke singles, another strand of tradition at the Cleckheaton, Yorkshire works where they were reputedly as 'economical' as Jack Benny, Panther had long been offering economy Villiers-engined models which, like the pre-war Red Panther, provided the ultimate cheapo machine. In our period, Panthers ended up being the heaviest of the lightweights, and having the last 99

2T-engined machines in production. The cynical would say that they became an excuse to use up stocks of existing components.

9E-engined Panthers began with the 4-speed 1956-1962 Model 10/4, with a Frank Leach-designed frame which, with variations in engine plates, would house all the company's two-strokes. The frame was fully welded, with a braced elliptical swinging-arm pivoting on Silentbloc bushes and controlled by non-adjustable Armstrong units angled to match the line of the toolboxes set in the well-panelled, pressed steel mid-section. This was another chunky continental style design, emphasised by the 3.25 x 18in tyres and wheels with their 5in brakes in full-width hubs. Actual weight of the 10/4 was 245lb. Reynolds-Earles front forks with Armstrong dampers went at the front end, a clever design with the tubes echoing the curves of the valanced mudguard so they looked like telescopics. On the singles they worked well. Finished in gold-lined maroon, the 10/4 was joined in 1957 by the 3-speed 10/3A and both got 6in brakes all round. Nothing much changed, other than a change of colour to red for 1960, until the finish in 1962.

The 2T-engined Panthers started with the confusingly numbered Model 35 in 1957. In the singles' running gear and finish, but weighing 290lb, the twins' output reportedly overstressed the leading link forks, causing some breakages, and the latter were soon strengthened. To a tester, they felt different but were sound, and were both comfortable and part of the excellent braking; the British Hub 6in brakes worked well, giving a stopping distance of 29ft from 30mph. 1958 saw an all-Pearl Grey Model 35 Sports version with chrome tank panels and mildly tuned engine, and for both twins there was a 7in front brake, with the forks modified so as to raise them.

1959 2T-engined Panther Model 35, with well-concealed leading-link forks and styling which, like several Brits of the period, owed something to the German DKW.

1959 brought the Model 45 with a 3T engine, and for all models the forks were strengthened, with a curved connecting tube above the pivot and a pair of strengthening gussets; the rear fork was strengthened too. The 45 was all red with chrome tank panels. It was joined in 1960 by the Model 50 Grand Sports with partial rear enclosure matched by a deep front mudguard. The Model 50 also featured Panther's heavyweight Model 120 singles' telescopic front fork as well as its 8in front brake, and at 333lb was the heaviest Villiers-powered bike ever! Only 230 were made. 1960 also saw the Model 35 get the rear enclosure and all the twins take to the Panther's middleweight Model 65/75 four-stroke's telescopic front end, though not the big brake.

Panthers were shortly in financial trouble, so 1962 saw the end of the standard Model 35 and of the Model 50. The 35 Sports went in 1963 but after a gap in production the standard 35 with its 6in front brake was back, presumably to use up existing stocks. 1964 was the last year for the Model 45, but it was joined again from April by the Model 35, and 1965 saw the beginning of the 2T Dynastart-engined 12-volt Model 35 ES, radically restyled as Red Panthers, as well as the same machine, as the 35 Sports, with a

1967 Model 35ES Sports 'Red Panther' twin with Siba electric start version of 2T. The last of all the production Villiers twin-engined models.

6-volt, 10:1 CR kickstart engine. These engines had been out of production for two years, and were in fact Ambassador stock acquired cheaply from DMW! These machines were painted red all over with kidney-shaped tank, chrome sports mudguards, siamesed exhaust systems (which in practice were noisy, caused back pressure problems and gunked up the silencer), flyscreen, turned-down bars, a frame with revised head angle and smaller triangular toolboxes. Front forks were again an adaptation of the ones on the Model 65/75 4-stroke middleweights, but it was a shame about the $5\frac{1}{2}$in front brake. Harsh but sporty, these machines lingered on until 1968, the last of the Villiers-engined twins.

Ownership of any of these models carries the benefit of membership of the Panther fraternity, known for their particular brand of benign weirdness. These are among the more durable of the lightweights. Prices should be around the Francis-Barnett mark, but capable of going a little higher due to the marque's mystique.

Royal Enfield

Normally associated with a fine range of 4-stroke singles and twins, the Redditch firm did enjoy one foray into the wonderful world of 2-strokes with their 250 Turbo Twin. Unfortunately it was 4T-engined, but still one of the best Villiers-engined motorcycles.

Introduced as an economy model in 1964 until 1966, at a time when the company was already in trouble, the Turbo Twin placed the 4T engine into the four-stroke 250 Clipper cycle parts. These included the Enfield open diamond swinging-arm frame where the engine itself sat as a stressed member between the single downtube and the rear frame. Despite undamped forks, non-adjustable Armstrongs, and an unbushed swinging-arm, this frame handled and held the road excellently, especially with the twin engine's low centre of gravity, and the 4T seemed to suit it, with the Turbo giving a unexpectedly turbine-smooth ride. The engine's proportions too suited the Enfield's cycle parts with their light-coloured top dual-seat and that year's slimmer $3\frac{1}{2}$ gallon petrol tank, in two-tone flame and cream finish.

In proven, strong Royal Enfield cycle parts, their 4T-engined Turbo Twin, built for just two years, is still one of the most desirable Villiers-engined roadsters.

This tank came with chrome, gold-lined 'eyebrow' side panels in the Turbo Twin Sports, which also fitted dropped bars and chromed mudguards. The 4T engine on test returned a very competitive 75mph top speed and could be cruised at 65, with only a grounding centre stand limiting the angle of lean, and 75mpg overall fuel consumption being another draw. A poor 6in front brake was not, but substitutes from the rest of the range are possible.

The standard model ran to the end of 1965, and the Sports finished, with all the other Royal Enfields bar the Interceptor Twins, at the end of 1966. These are desirable machines of which around a thousand were made, and prices can be on the high side despite the fact that Enfields generally don't make good money, so it's difficult to say what prices can be expected. Say £300-£450 for tidy runners, and a little more for really good ones. The cycle part interchange with the rest of the Enfield range make this an easier restoration proposition than many.

Sun

This small concern run by the Parkes family in Aston, Birmingham had a good reputation for the quality of its finish; they were allowed to advertise with the phrase 'The Rolls-Royce of lightweight motorcycles' by RR themselves. Virtually hand-built and rather expensive, their oddly-styled Villiers-engined roadsters are rarities today.

The 9E-engine Wasp came in either 3- or 4-speed versions from 1957 to 1959. On a single downtube, bolted-up loop frame with swinging-arm rear suspension with Armstrong dampers, a rear enclosure with three long ribs blended with a deeply

1958 9E-engined Sun Wasp, run-of-the-mill single, but well finished.

valanced rear mudguard, and was matched by a well-valanced front guard which, together with shrouds, concealed the Armstrong short leading link front suspension. Finished in two-tone grey with optional chromed tank panels, the Wasp rode on 3 x 19in wheels with 5in brakes in full-width hubs, front and rear. All that, with the leading link forks, added up to a weight of 244lb. I have never ridden one or read a Sun road-test, but there was a competition version of the Wasp and Don Morley, who owned one, rated it highly, finding the steering geometry, albeit for trials use, admirable, and the expensive finish durable.

The 2T-engined machine from 1957 to 1959 was called the Wasp Twin **103** before it changed to the Overlander, which indicates that all was similar to the single except for a 280lb weight, a slightly longer wheelbase to accommodate the twin's larger crankcase, and a gold-lined Italian Red colour scheme from 1958, together with 6in front brakes. For 1959 the rear enclosure for both single and twin lost its three ribs, and was further extended to shroud the rear dampers. Then motorcycle production ceased and soon after Sun, like Norman, sold out to Raleigh Cycles.

Extremely uncommon but not in a coveted way, prices for any Sun that turns up should be low, from £150 for a single and £200 for a twin.

Summary

DMW and Greeves are at the top of the list on all counts, but priced accordingly, and for the Greeves in every case and DMW in some, with unorthodox forks to maintain. The stylish later Ambassadors would be pleasing to own, as would a Panther or the Royal Enfield twin, each with their different associations, but all three solidly built with telescopic forks, and good handlers. A Cotton's handling alone for some would outweigh some poor styling and the comparative complications of the Armstrong fork. The roadsters under consideration here use the later version of the Armstrong fork, with an alloy top yoke rather than the earlier steel type, bolted-on headlamp nacelle rather than welded-on brackets, and longer dampers. The sports Cottons alone featured, from 1961 on, a bracing loop round the wheel. While the forks are not difficult to service, even second hand spares are not common, and you will probably have to turn up your own bushes etc.

The more unusual marques, Dot, Excelsior, Norman and Sun, all had their virtues, and if one presented itself at the right price, could probably be ridden with make-do cycle parts while the pukkah ones were sought out, for the uncommon nature of these roadsters would surely encourage restoration. And that leaves the two related major makes, Francis-Barnett and James, both tele-forked and now as then, representing the best all round choice. The only exception is the last Sports Cruiser/Sports Superswift, though even then their looks have an appeal. Otherwise, though the handling was respectable rather than outstanding, the sound design, build quality and convenience for spares and cycle parts due to the numbers built, must leave the 'Practical' crown to these Francis-Barnetts, with their James cousins a close second.

Villiers 9E and 2T-engined machines today

This section should begin with a budgetary word of warning, passed on by Nick Kelly, an arch Villiers enthusiast who has owned literally dozens of these devices. It is a common mistake to think that because the Villiers-powered lightweights were often economy models in their time, and can usually be purchased for very reasonable sums today, they will be cheaper than anything else to get running and on the road. It costs as much to have a James Captain's wheel rebuilt as it does that of a T160 Trident. So think hard before selecting a machine and don't be seduced by dirt cheap non-runners unless your budget allows for fettling them. All the prices in the preceding section are for privately sold runners or something very close to it. As Kelly confirms, you can easily spend £900 doing up a twin, of which even the best examples will be pushed to fetch more than £500-£600 when selling. The singles may be slow, but there is less to go wrong with them.

Buy nothing unless it's at least 80% present, however poor the condition, particularly in terms of mudguards and the very varied panelling involved. You need a correct set of tinware, which you will otherwise have to borrow, so that you can get new items made up in glass fibre — steel and aluminium are too expensive. Nick Kelly says that there are plenty of people working in fibreglass, in the field of yachting, canoeing, etc., who can help and who can be found in the *Yellow Pages*. Though the cost of a mould can be £200-£250, this would be for a complex moulding, and include a batch of say 10 to 20 finished products in the price. Small, simple moulds can be far cheaper, from £20 to £50. Once a mould has been made up, extra sets can be produced to sell to fellow sufferers. The mighty Panther Owners Club did this for the Model 35/50 side panels, which sold at £40. Hunting in autojumbles for second-hand originals is slower but cheaper, though unlikely to be successful for rarer models. Autocycle is always worth a try too, especially for James and Francis-Barnett bits. With all these two-strokes, it is particularly important to have a place to store things and work, as accumulating spares to swap and non-runners to cannibalise is the way to run one on a budget.

One problem with buying a Villiers-engined machine can be identifying exactly what its engine is. Villiers engine numbers were carried on a plate riveted to the inner half of the primary chaincase. This plate may have been lost; or another chaincase may have been used to replace the original, due to damage etc., so the numbers on it may not apply to the engine to which it is attached. To discover the actual capacity and the number of gears in an engine under scrutiny, removing the head and measuring up may be necessary, as well as working the gearbox. Villier's change pattern was up for first, then down for second, third, etc.

Once you possess a Villiers, one benefit is their honest sturdiness and the fact that they can be worked on with few special tools. The top end can be removed with the engine in situ, and the same goes for work on the clutch, final drive sprocket, contact breaker and flywheel assembly. However, detaching the gearbox means having the engine out of the frame. One special tool was the famous Villiers Hammertight spanner. One end of this fits over the flywheel magneto retaining nut, while the other is both shaped and made strong enough to take a healthy whack with a hammer. This loosens off the nut, which as it turns slackens off and then tightens again, hence continuing to pull off the magneto's rotor. A hefty ring spanner, preferably with an extension, will do instead of the Hammertight. Another useful tool is a clutch centre holder for use in meshing the teeth of the

engine and clutch sprockets while the main retaining nuts are slackened, but this is essentially just an old clutch plate to which a handle and legs have been welded or bolted, and it can be fabricated.

Opposite top: *1958 Sun Overlander twin, with the semi-enclosed style then fashionable.*

Opposite bottom: **Twin power allows outfits like this sporting one. But the Greeves alone would probably be outside our budget.**

Within the engine the small end bush often needs renewing, and the gearchange and kickstart return springs should be renewed as a matter of course. In any Villiers engine which has stood for more than a year, the fibre crankcase seals will have dried up, and begun to leak, so that the two-stroke's necessary crankcase compression is lost. Renewal of the seals, plus new piston rings and a good decoke, should set things right. However, signs to watch for then are excessive vibration and rough running, which can be caused by wear in the main bearings. Many miles before the bearings fail, the shaft will drop slightly in relation to them, allowing air past the seals again, to cause difficult starting and rough, spluttering running because the mixture will then be too weak. Main bearing renewal will be the only permanent cure. If a crank needs rebuilding, Alpha Bearings undertake this, even for the rebuild experts, DMW.

On Villiers electrics, the good bit about the flywheel magneto is that, like any magneto, it provides ignition not dependent on the state of the battery. The problem is that it can be affected by the build-up of heat, meaning that the machine will start, run for a while and then fade, and refuse to start again while warm. This is usually due to loss of magnetism from age, which can eventually affect starting in any condition. The answer is to have the magnets remagnetised; a Bristol firm (see Useful Information) has the necessary special machine and rig, and will do this, at the time of writing, for 75p a magnet.

A further electrical problem can be the vulnerability to water of the Bakelite moulding contains the HT contact pad and spring which emerges from the front of the right-side crankcase cover facing forward. Don Morley, in his British two-stroke trials book, with competition conditions in mind, advocates drilling the cover and re-routing this, but for the road, sealing the Bakelite pick-up holder around with plasticine should do the trick. Another problem may be signalled by a high-speed misfire that gets worse although starting and revving are unaffected, which usually means the condenser is on the way out. Replacing the small Villiers points condenser with a larger car one, remotely mounted beneath the tank, is another possibility. Finally, the Westinghouse half-wave rectifiers specified for the 2T's rectified-lighting system are now unavailable, but the substitution of cheap modern 200-volt 10-amp diodes — two of them, because the Westinghouse contained two diode elements — should work, and indeed produce a higher charging rate.

Once your Villiers-engined machine is up and running, you can expect **107** around 60mpg from the 250 twin, dropping to around 40 with hard usage, while the 9E/10E should return at least around the 80mpg mark. Nick Kelly finds that all Villiers engines run happily on unleaded fuel, and he uses modern, low-ash synthetic oils in a 25:1 mix, the modern oil's efficiency allowing the use of less oil than the makers recommended. He also favours a drop of the Teflon-based Slick 50 additive for easing internals. SAE 30 is good for gearbox oil, though 20/50 will also do, and SAE 20 for the primary chaincase. Spark plugs are Champion L7 or NGK B5HS for the 2T, and Champion L5 for both the 9E/10E and the 3T /4T twins.

Spares have already been mentioned, but one point is that the Villiers own-brand exhaust pipes and silencers fitted on the 2T-engined machines can be replaced by those from a Honda CB 72, which are the right shape and have stronger flanges; though these are rare themselves today, and you should check whether the latter marry with individual machines. Otherwise Armours (see Section 3 Useful Information) do a general purpose pipe and silencer for the Villiers singles, though some DIY finishing work may be necessary to match a particular machine; the same goes for their

A shot that suggests all the appeal of the Villiers twin, as the late Bob Currie powers a 1962 Francis-Barnett Cruiser 89 through a bend.

universal mudguards. If you want to substitute an Amal carburettor for convenience on your 9E, DMW can provide a suitable adaptor inlet stub.

Both engines when running right are good for extended mileages of the 35-50,000 mile order. DMW will rebuild a single engine for around £200 and a twin for about £300, and for the singles at least the figure can be less if they are found to be in good condition in some areas. Alf Snell (see Useful Information) also undertakes this service. Properly set up and often fitted in traditionally highly substantial cycle parts (Francis-Barnett, Panther, etc.) both single and twin can make robust everyday mounts and provide practical touring tools as well. Recent visits to Portugal and Turkey left me impressed with the way that 2-stroke singles and twins respectively (Jawas built under licence in the case of Turkey) provided the basic daily transport for the majority of rural road-users. Many of the Villiers-engines bikes were supplying just that in Britain 30 years ago. 'Agricultural' may have connotations of crude and heavy, but it can also mean strong and reliable.

A typical 9E/10E-engined machine: Francis-Barnett Falcon 81 (1958): Technical Data

Engine

Bore, mm	59	
Stroke, mm	72	
Capacity, cc	197	
Compression ratio	7.25:1	
Ignition	Flywheel magneto	
Carburettor	Villiers S25	

Transmission (3 speed)

Sprockets

Engine	20	
Clutch	43	
Gearbox	18	
Rear wheel	48	
Top gear	6.07:1	
2nd gear	8.13:1	
1st gear	15.48:1	
Chain (front)	3/8 in x 0.225 in	
Chain (rear)	$\frac{1}{2}$ in x 0.205 in 122 pitches	

Brakes

Diam. front, (in)	5
Diam. rear, (in)	5

Tyres

Size front, (in)	3.25 x 18
Size rear, (in)	3.25 x 18

Electrical

Battery	12 ah
Headlamp (diam. in)	6
Voltage	6

Miscellaneous

Fuel, Imp. gall.	$2\frac{3}{4}$
Seat height (in)	31
Wheelbase (in)	$49\frac{3}{4}$
Ground clearance (in)	6
Dry weight (lb)	220 approx

A typical 2T-engined machine: Ambassador Supreme (1958): Technical Data

Engine

Bore, mm	50
Stroke, mm	63.5
Capacity, cc	249
Compression ratio	8.2:1
Ignition	Flywheel magneto
Carburettor	Villiers S22/2

Transmission
Sprockets

Engine	20
Clutch	43
Gearbox	18
Rear wheel	51
Top gear	6.09:1
3rd gear	8.04:1
2nd gear	11.57:1
1st gear	18.64:1

Chain (front)	$\frac{3}{8}$ x 0.225 in
Chain (rear)	$\frac{1}{2}$ x 0.305 in 121 pitches

Brakes

Diam. front, (in)	6
Diam/ rear, (in)	6

Tyres

Size front, (in)	3.25 x 17
Size rear, (in)	3.25 x 17

Electrical

Battery	8 ah
Headlamp (diam. in)	7
Voltage	6

Miscellaneous

Fuel, Imp. gall	$3\frac{1}{4}$
Seat height (in)	30
Wheelbase (in)	50
Ground clearance (in)	$5\frac{1}{2}$
Dry weight (lb)	260 approx

Villiers: Useful Information

Books

The Villiers Engine by D.E. Browning (Pearsons, o/p)
The Book of the Villiers Engine by Cyril Grange (Pitmans, o/p)
Villiers Singles and Twins by Roy Bacon (Osprey, £8.95)
Greeves by Rob Carrick and Mick Walker (Osprey, £14.95)
Classic British Two-Stroke Trials Bikes by Don Morley (Osprey, £10.95)
Restoring Motorcycles 4: Two-Stroke Engines by Roy Bacon (Osprey £9.95)

Clubs

The British Two-Stroke Club: Membership Secretary, Alan Abrahams, 38 Charles Drive, Cuxton, Rochester, Kent ME2 1DR. Eligible for VMCC insurance scheme.
Greeves Riders Association: Peter Smith, 6 George's Road, Winsford, Cheshire.
Francis-Barnett Owners Club: Cher Gardner, 58 Knowle Road, Totterdown,

Bristol.

Dot Owners Club, Eric J. Watson, 31 Proppshall Drive, Failsworth, Manchester M35 0WB.
Panther Owners Club: Angie and Jonathan Jones, Coopers Cottage, Park Lane, Castle Camps, Cambridge, CB1 6SR.

Shops

Smoothline Motorcycle Components, Tyffynon, Crickhowell, Powys NP8 1RU (Tel: 0874 730076) 9E spares, competition orientated.
Chris Williams, Autocycle, 50 Church Street, Moxley, Wednesbury, West Midlands WS10 8RE (Tel: 0902 45528).
John Burdon, Frankfield Road, Gt. Ayton, Middlesbrough, Cleveland.
DMW Motorcycles, Valley Road Works, Sedgeley, Dudley, Birmingham (Tel: 0902 880351) Single and twin spares and rebuilds.
Meeten and Ward, 360 Kingston Road, Ewell, Surrey (Tel: 01-393 5139).
Terry Silvester Motorcycles, Springlane Mills, Woodhead Road, Holmfirth, Huddersfield, Yorks. HD7 1PR (Tel: 0484 683665).
Alf Snell, 17 Drysdale Avenue, Chingford, London E4 (Tel: 01-524 7688). Engineering services and rebuilds, also spares. Callers by arrangement only.
Bristol Ignition and Dynamo Co., 27 Stokes Croft, Bristol 1, Avon (Tel: 0272 249646): remagnetising Villiers flywheels.

Chapter Ten

The Ariel Leader/Arrow

The revolutionary all-enclosed Ariel Leader 250 two-stroke twin, and its stripped Arrow cousin, only just scrape into this lightweight volume.

Not because of their avoirdupois — the Leader weighed 300lb dry, though the figure rose to 330lb when all the many available options were fitted, and the Arrows around 275lb, all similar to Villiers 2T-engined machines. Nor because of an impractical nature or any lack of performance — the faired Leaders were good for around 70mph, while the Arrows went to around 75 and the Super Sports 'Golden Arrow' just saw 80mph.

No, the debar for the Leader and Arrows is price, and for that reason this section will be briefer than the other two. Though not specially cherished, they are both still rated enough to fetch around £350-£400 for a runner, with the fully-equipped Leader's combination of quaintness and genuine Hall-of-Fame status due to its many progressive features making a well-finished example worth almost double that sum.

The design was often inspired, and the production run was of some 36,000 models, roughly split between the two variants and produced in around seven years. But the Leader/Arrows with their pressed-steel panelling and their flashy, sometimes compromise styling — the engine was never intended to be exposed, the unfaired models being an afterthought created by market forces - never really won the hearts of British motorcyclists, which perhaps explains why they are not worth more today. Their ingenious conveniences and acceptable power and handling had to be balanced against a poor gearbox, very poor brakes, some crankshaft problems, awkward cold starting and accessibility, and a two-stroke engine which always seemed to be the smokiest on the scene.

Nevertheless, Arrows, particularly Golden Arrows (so called because of their polychromatic gold and ivory finish) are about the most sporting mounts featured in these pages, while a Leader is the epitome among two-strokes of the Sensible ideal — it's often overlooked, because of very

Quite a triumph in its own right - the fully-equipped new Ariel Leader for 1958.

different ambience and styling, that the Leader with its beam frame and enclosure owes much in concept to one of the few other all-new postwar designs, Velocette's little LE. The Leader tried to make good the LE's deficiency in power, and to incorporate the qualities of the market-leading scooters — two-stroke simplicity and zip, weather protection, small (16in) wheels, two-tone colour schemes, etc.

113

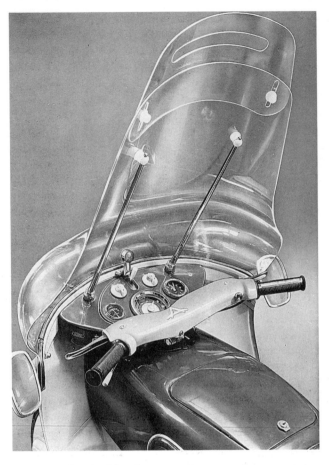

The fact that Ariel did not succeed, as we shall see, was due more to the politics of the BSA group of which they formed a part than to any fundamental deficiencies in the design.

Leader's optional windscreen extension, purpose-built mirrors, eight-day clock, two-way windscreen, parking light - you've got to get them all.

Today a Leader in particular can offer a practical and rather dignified conveyance, as well as an absorbing pastime: tracking down each of the fourteen or so optional extras — the eight-day clock, the chrome rear bumper bar with reflectors, the zipbags for inside the panniers — that went to make up a fully-equipped version. When you've got them all, go to the head of the class.

Ariel Leader/Arrow History

The Leader, introduced in July 1958, was the last work of Ariel's great designer, Val Page. The company itself was known for an honest, well-finished range of four-strokes including the Edward Turner-designed Square Four, Page's Red Hunter singles, and a 650 twin based on the A10 from BSA, who had taken over Ariel in 1944.

With big singles on the wane and BSA-Triumph having the parallel twin four-stroke market covered, to their credit Ariel in the mid-fifties undertook some market research among riders before turning the company in a completely new direction. The one thing that consistently emerged from the research was the desire for a middleweight 250 two-stroke twin, like the contemporary Continental Jawa-CZ and DKW. Allying this to scooter trends and to production economy by the use of die-casting and pressing for major components, Page and his assistant Bernard Knight evolved the beam-framed Leader.

The engine's 54 x 54mm cylinder dimensions and their 45° angle of forward inclination were identical to those of another European two-stroke twin, the excellent German 250 Adler, but Page's design differed in many respects and resulted in a commendably narrow unit, as well as one low enough to fit beneath the beam frame with its dummy petrol tank. Designed as a sleek whole, another Leader first was the use of plastics in several applications. The end result was genuine weather protection from the acceptable-looking legshields and windscreen, without compromising the motorcycle virtues of handling, from the stiff swinging-arm chassis, low centre of gravity and trailing-link forks, and acceptable 70mph performance. As Ariel's advertising put it, 'Why choose a motorcycle or a scooter when you can have both?'

A well-kept secret, the Leader on its launch in July 1958 (a good year for the industry) was bang in line with current trends, as the British motorcycle industry struggled back against the scooters that were outselling them. In two-tone grey and blue or red, plus whitewall tyres, and with unit-construction, small wheels and an enclosed mid-section, it echoed Triumph's trend-setting 1957 350 3TA twin, but surpassed the latter in offering scooter-style luggage capacity, and set several other useful firsts, like the optional direction indicators, and a stop-light operated by the front as well as the rear brake.

The Leader was a convincing package and the British public fairly soon reacted positively. By 1960 sales were brisk, production briefly rose to 1600 a month, and versions were sold to some police forces.

Ariel Leader's scooter appeal - but the luggage compartment's unreliable lock made leaving your handbag in there unwise.

But the picture soon darkened for several reasons. First, the distinctive nature of motorcycles as opposed to scooter buyers asserted itself. This was particularly true for young riders, who statistically made up an increasing share of the 115 market as two-wheelers shifted from being utility transport to leisure items. At home there was a fairly rapid reaction against enclosed motorcycles; and in America, increasingly the British industry's main export market, neither pressed steel nor two-strokes were ever accepted.

Secondly, internal shifts within the BSA group had brought Triumph's Edward Turner to the head of their Automotive Division, and Turner had a habit of favouring his own creations. While too late to interfere with the Leader launch, he certainly curbed further necessary development work on the Ariel twin. 1960, the year learners were restricted to machines of 250cc or under, saw the challenge of the youth market met by Ariel with

Police version of the unfaired Ariel Arrow, with crash bars and big battery to cope with the radio gear.

the gawky but quite effective unfaired version, the Arrow; but it also saw all production at Ariel's Selly Oak factory turned over to the two-strokes — and, quite suddenly, the start of a decade-long downturn in the domestic motorcycle market.

116   From then on, Turner and others quashed development not only of

the Leader/Arrow, but of several hopeful, potentially revivifying company projects, including a tube-framed version of the twin that could have sold in America; Hermann Meier's racing version which came 7th in the 1960 Lightweight TT; and an amazing flat in-line four cylinder prototype, uncannily similar in layout to BMW's twenty years later K-series. After a couple of lean years, Ariel's order book had reportedly sunk to just 15 machines when the company was removed from its Selly Oak home, and production shifted to BSA's Small Heath works.

There it was only a matter of time, since without any further development the twins' unsatisfactory Burman gearbox (and the lack of a fifth or sixth cog), its poor brakes and smoke-prone petroil system (looking increasingly old-fashioned in the face of Japanese pumped lubrication systems), plus detail shortcomings like thief-friendly locks on the parcel compartment and steering head, rot-prone seats and poor accessibility, etc., all went unattended. A sleeved-down 200 Arrow version in 1964, for insurance benefits, hardly stemmed the tide, and the finish came late in 1965, the excuse being Burman's abrupt shift to car gearbox manufacture. Selly Oak's twin had deserved better, embodying some progressive ideas and real potential, as well as being reliable enough in standard form.

Ariel Leader/Arrow Development History

Ariel's 180 degree 249cc two-stroke twin engine featured a single Amal Monobloc carburettor (dictated by a structural member on the frame), and piston porting. It was built in unit with a scaled-down version of the 4-speed Burman CP gearbox, though this occupied a separate chamber within the alloy crankcase.

The latter, unusually for a British machine, was a single die-casting, unsplit. Each crank chamber was accessible, Scott-style, by a 'door' in the side, so that the bottom end, like the gearbox, could be worked on with the engine in place. Since the alloy heads and iron cylinders with their generous angled finning were separate, they too could be stripped individually. Compression on these early engines was 8.25:1, and power output 16bhp at 6400rpm.

The crankshaft ran on three ball races, one at each end and one cleverly mounted in the dividing wall between the two crank chambers, with a pair of oil seals mounted back to back with it. The crankshaft itself was formed in two halves, with an ingenious taper and end-key coupling, and featured an external flywheel in the primary chaincase. Primary drive was by a single-row chain, and the clutch was an unusual design with corrugated-pattern drum and plates. Electrics were via a crankshaft-mounted Lucas RM13/15 alternator, unconventionally positioned on the right. All-up engine weight was 84lb.

The engine was suspended by three mounting brackets, the rear one doubling as an air-silencer chamber, from the Leader's backbone, which was a large section beam formed by two 20 gauge steel pressings welded together. Within it, positioned beneath the hinged dualseat, was the $2\frac{1}{2}$ gallon **117** petrol tank. At the rear, the beam widened and forked to form the upper mounting for the Armstrong non-adjustable rear suspension units. At the front it swept up to embrace the steering-head tube for the trailing-link forks, with Armstrong dampers running up inside the legs concealed by pressed-steel spats. The limbs themselves pivoted on nylon bushes, and no steering yoke was fitted, since the forks only extended up as far as the cup-and-cone steering head. The handlebars were mounted on the central steering column, and concealed beneath a scooter-style shroud.

This basic structure was then shrouded by means of eight main steel pressings, including a hinged, raisable tail section, for access to the full

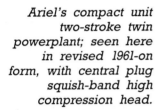

Ariel's compact unit two-stroke twin powerplant; seen here in revised 1961-on form, with central plug squish-band high compression head.

width alloy hub q.d. rear wheel. A left panel fastened by five screws concealed the contact-breakers, primary chaincase and carburettor, and the right panel required the kickstart and gearchange pedals' removal before it could be detached. The dummy tank fitted with kneegrips had a lockable parcel compartment within. A windscreen with blisters for hand protection sat in a rubber-lined channel at the top of the frontal fairing, with the 6in headlamp mounted in a further pressing protruding from it, and adjustable by a knob on the instrument panel. Optional steel panniers very much completed the picture, and at this stage were the only way of benefiting from the (also optional) direction indicators, which at the rear were built into the panniers. Finish was two tone, with light grey for the lower half, front fork and mudguard, and the rest in Oriental Blue or Cherokee Red, all with matching seats and whitewall tyres.

Remarks

The early Leader was a basically sound design, and set up as a tourer/commuter, it generally returned good service. One potentially weak spot was the coupled crankshaft, but this only became a problem as output rose. The gearbox was more of a permanent problem, with an over-long lever providing rough and stiff changes, false neutrals and a big gap between 3rd and top.

The Leader's ingenious rider-friendly intentions sometimes fell down in practice. Finish was poor, and the dualseat with its plywood base prone

1961 Ariel Arrow, stripped version of the twin with central plug cylinder head.

to rotting. The carburettor tickler and cold-start rod had to protrude through the panelling, and the latter never worked well despite a 1960 mod to give a half-on position. Fitting a throttle cable was awkward due to the proximity of the carburettor to the frame, and adjusting the carburettor needed a double-jointed hand — yet a lack of accurate adjustment could cause seizure.

The electrics were barely adequate, with the headlight poor and the contact-breakers flimsy and prone to going quickly out of adjustment. The 6in brakes' poor performance was another serious minus point, and the early alloy brake plates would sometimes prove prone to cracking. Finally both the steering-lock with its nylon mounting and the lock on the parcel compartment (which also contained the catch to raise the dualseat) were weak, while the windscreen proved vulnerable and expensive to replace.

1959

A further finish option became available this year, Battleship Grey upper paintwork with a black dualseat. Mid-year, the connecting rods were changed from 'H' to oval section.

1960

This year marked the introduction of the unfaired *Arrow* version, with the engine unit exposed. The timing side crankcase cover, front fork inspection cover and dummy racing-style 2½ gallon pannier tank were all finished in Dark Seal Grey, the remainder of the paintwork being in light Admiralty Grey. At the rear of the machine the valanced mudguard, number plate and light, supported cantilever fashion, were fastened to the tail of a beam section, chrome plated brackets being employed to support the silencers. The handlebars were fully exposed and of the conventional type. The **119** headlamp was supported by extensions on the dummy fuel tank which contained within its luggage compartment the tool tray, arranged to have storage space beneath it. Circular tank badges were fitted, one of which was removable to provide access to the rectifier. The absence of the top pressing reduced seat height from 31 to 28½ inches. The overall weight was 270lb and the top speed 75mph.

1961

From mid-1961 both the Leader and the Arrow used cast iron hubs and 6 x 1¼ in brake drums, the brake shoes being fabricated from heavy pressings and fitted with serrated, pressed operating levers without fulcrum adjusters. These replaced their earlier alloy counterparts. An air strangler was provided with a notch for a half-open position and the carburettor jet spray tube top was slanted toward the engine. The fuel filler cap was also modified.

1961 also marked the introduction of the *Super Sports Golden Arrow* model, distinguished by its gold-coloured dummy fuel tank and rear number plate housing. The remainder of the machine was finished in light Admiralty Grey, with a chrome plated toolbox lid, timing side crankcase cover, lifting handles, air filter body and front fork inspection covers. The overall effect was enhanced by red handlebar grips, a black seat and whitewall tyres, as well as by a flyscreen, dropped handlebars and ball-ended levers. Engine-wise, a larger Amal 1 inch Monobloc carburettor was fitted and a redesigned cylinder head used with slightly revised finning, a central spark plug and a squish band that provided a 10:1 compression ratio. This new cylinder head was also now specified for the Leader and Arrow models. It increased the power of the Leader and Arrow to 17.5bhp at 6750rpm, the Golden Arrow claiming 20.2bhp at 6650rpm, with a top speed of 80mph.

All models now featured a modified front brake anchorage, a fuel tank enlarged to hold 3 gallons, brake hubs given three external ribs to improve rigidity and, from mid-year, a front brake plate fitted with a water-excluding flange. Other modifications comprised revised clutch springs, Arrow-type silencers for the Leader with baffle tube guide vanes to impart a circular motion to the exhaust gases, a reduction in size of the carburettor main jet from 170 to 140, and provision for fitting flashing direction indicators to the rear mudguard.

Remarks

The Arrow, and especially the Golden Arrow, redressed the problem of the touring Leader's lack of youth appeal. Brash, inelegant machines, the Arrow's 75mph plus took the machine to the limit of its handling and in the case of the Golden Arrow could stress the engine and reduce operational life. Even so, they were what the market demanded. Unfortunately, the modification to the brakes, except for the waterproofing, did little to help make them more effective. Development effectively ceased from this point on.

Touring, in this delightful period picture, but more often seen scratching - Ariel's Super Sports Golden Arrow for 1961.

1962

On all models the previously used light Admiralty Grey lower paintwork areas were changed to an ivory finish, the Arrow being available only in black and ivory, this finish being an option for the Leader. A Lucas RM18 121 alternator was now fitted and the wiring harness modified, using a new key-operated ignition switch. The front brake plate was now stiffened by the addition of internal ribs, a water-excluding flange fitted to the rear brake plate and 'anti-squeal' springs fitted to the brake shoes.

1963

A further option became available for the finish of the Arrow's upper paintwork areas — Cherokee Red.

1964

For this year the *Arrow 200* made its debut, the engine reduced in capacity by sleeving down the cylinder bores to 48.5mm to give a cubic capacity of 199.5cc. A smaller bore $\frac{13}{16}$ inch carburettor was fitted and the overall gearing lowered by the use of a 49 tooth rear wheel sprocket. The new model was available in an ivory and Aircraft Blue or an ivory and British Racing Green finish, the Arrow being available in ivory with Flamboyant Red, Aircraft Blue or British Racing Green, or all black.

1966

The Arrow was dropped from production by the beginning of the year and by the end of the year production of the remaining models had been stopped too.

The Ariel Leader/Arrows Today

The Ariel two-strokes are valid performers on today's roads, with the exception of their brakes. The spares situation is good for the engine and gearbox, and not at all bad for the cycle parts, with some gaps in the panelling and trim. There is a good Ariel specialist supplier, Draganfly in Suffolk, run by brothers Roger and Graham Gwynn, and as well as keeping tabs on available spares and getting some manufactured, they offer useful engine work, such as an exchange crankshaft reconditioning service.

Those awkward parts include some of the rubber trim, Arrow tankbadges and rear mudguards, Leader front panels and *right - hand* legshields (of course — it's always right-hand components — will they all turn up one day in Australia, I wonder?). The Armstrong rear suspension units for these models had a unique car-type top fixing, with a single central stud marrying with the frame via steel and rubber washers, and these units are also unobtainable today, though new ones for the trailing link front forks can be had.

When buying, the condition of these units are among points to watch for. Others include the earlier alloy hubs which are crack-prone; their linings are also in short supply. Check the frame behind the steering head area for accident damage. Poor starting and smoking are endemic, but exceptionally bad instances of both these features, as with the Villiers two-strokes, will indicate main bearings on the way out so that the crank is wearing through the seals.

The final version of Ariel's two-stroke, the cut-price Arrow 200 for 1964-5.

Of the consumables, the 16in tyres present no problems, one acceptable modern equivalent being the Michelin M38, though no authentic-looking ribbed front covers are available, nor any safe whitewalled one. Plugs are Champion N4 or NGK B7ES, like the Bantam. Unleaded petrol should be fine, and around 70mpg was normal for a Leader, dropping somewhat for an Arrow if driven hard. With modern low-ash oil, in Draganfly's estimation the mixture can be slimmed from the originally recommended 32:1 to 40:1.

This may help with the enduringly memorable visual aspect of an Ariel twin on the move, namely the smokescreens they used to trail behind them; after the 1960 silencer was fitted, their internals gave the exhaust gases a spiral motion, so the Ariels laid twin curls of smoke.

Otherwise the Leader and Arrow provide a brisk ride up to 60mph even after relatively high mileages (except for the highly tuned Golden Arrow), though the engines need to be revved for best results. Handling is more than adequate up to 60, but beyond that can feature weaving and choppiness, especially on fast bumpy bends; as with many British four-stroke twins, powering through corners and never shutting off is the correct technique.

While the ride is smooth enough when the engine is well set up, the contact breakers easily go out of adjustment and are fiddly to work on, which often leads to a rougher engine. The gearchange is rough at the **123** best of times and the selector spring fragile. As mentioned, some maintenance chores can be fiddly, and overall this is probably a machine for the rider with a fair degree of mechanical expertise. But if they do suit, the Arrows provide you with just about the swiftest, and the Leader in its way one of the most stylish, of all the British lightweights.

Ariel Leader (1958) Technical Data
Engine

Bore (mm)	54
Stroke (mm)	54
Capacity (cc)	249
Compression ratio	8.25:1
Ignition	Coil
Carburettor	Amal type 375 Monobloc

Transmission
Sprockets

Engine	22
Clutch	50
Gearbox	18
Rear wheel	47
Top gear (internal ratios)	1.0
3rd gear	1.31
2nd gear	1.86
1st gear	3.2
Chain (front)	$\frac{3}{8}$ in x 0.225in. 70 pitches
Chain (rear)	$\frac{1}{2}$ in x $\frac{5}{16}$ in. 113 pitches

Brakes

Diam. Front, (in)	6
Diam. Rear, (in)	6

Tyres

Size Front, (in)	3.25 x 16
Size Rear, (in)	3.25 x 16

Electrical

Battery	13ah
Headlamp (diam. in)	6
Voltage	6

Miscellaneous

Fuel, Imp. (gall)	2.5
Seat height (in)	30
Width (in)	24.5
Length (in)	73.5
Ground clearance (in.)	5
Dry weight (lb)	300
	(330 with all options)

Ariel Leader/Arrow: Engine numbers

Engine and frame numbers were carried on a plate riveted on near the petrol filler-cap beneath the seat. The Leader/Arrows always featured a T-prefix to their numbers, and used separate suffixes for the different models, as follows:

	Engine No. suffix
Leader	A
Leader (after October 1960, new cylinder head)	B
Arrow	S
Arrow (after October 1960, new cylinder head)	T
Arrow Super Sports	G
Arrow 200	H

Month, Year	Model	Engine
July, 1958	Leader	T101A
December 1959	Arrow	T9165S
October 1960	Leader	T17200A/T17591B
	Arrow	T17200S/T17441T
	Super Sports	T20384G
September 1961	Leader	T26293B
	Arrow	T26293T
	Super Sports	T26293G
September 1963	Leader	T32800B
	Arrow	T32800T
	Super Sports	T32800G
January 1964	Arrow	T33995T
April 1964	Arrow 200	T33701H
September 1964	Leader	T34700B
	Sports	T34725G
	Arrow 200	T34650H
August 1965	Leader	T35462B
	Sports	T35425G
	Arrow 200	T35506H

(Both the Ariel Owners Club and Draganfly hold more comprehensive engine and frame number lists and despatch records, and can date most machines to within a year.)

Ariel Leader/Arrow: Useful Information

Books

Ariel - The Postwar Models by Roy Bacon (Osprey £10.95).
British Motor Cycles since 1950 Vol I by Steve Wilson (PSL, £7.95). 125

BLACK AND WHITE pic.fig

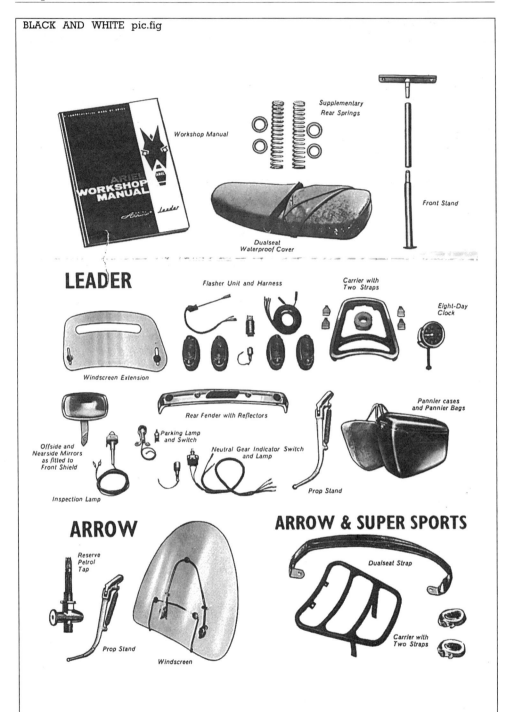

Workshop Manual

Supplementary Rear Springs

Front Stand

Dualseat Waterproof Cover

LEADER

Flasher Unit and Harness

Carrier with Two Straps

Eight-Day Clock

Windscreen Extension

Rear Fender with Reflectors

Pannier cases and Pannier Bags

Offside and Nearside Mirrors as fitted to Front Shield

Parking Lamp and Switch

Neutral Gear Indicator Switch and Lamp

Prop Stand

Inspection Lamp

ARROW

Reserve Petrol Tap

Prop Stand

Windscreen

ARROW & SUPER SPORTS

Dualseat Strap

Carrier with Two Straps

The full range of optional extras for the Leader, Arrow and Sports 200 models.

The Ariel Story by Peter Hartley (Argus Books, o/p).
The Book of the Ariel Leader and Arrow by W. C. Haycraft (Pitmans, o/p).

A selection of reproduced riders' handbooks and parts lists from Bruce Main-Smith, PO Box 20, Leatherhead, Surrey (Tel: 0372 375616).

Clubs
Ariel Motorcycle Owners Club, Mike Taylor, Harrow House, Woolscott, Rugby, Warwickshire, CV23 8DB.
British Two Stroke Club, see Chapter 9 Useful Information.

Shops
Draganfly Motorcycles, The Old Town Maltings, Broad Street, Bungay, Suffolk NR35 1EE (Tel: 0986 4798): Ariel specialists.
TC Motorcycles, 62 Northfield Road, Harborne, Birmingham (Tel: 021-779 6213).

Chapter Eleven

Gear, paperwork and shops

Having got hold of an old British lightweight, money will probably soon be on your mind. So we shall restate our purpose — getting the whole project on the road for under £500. We are assuming that around £200 has been spent on a near-enough runner. After that, allow about a third again for work and probably some necessary renewables, like a rear chain at £10, a new battery from around £15, or a tyre at around £35 complete with rim tape and inner tube. Some people enjoy getting the last mile out of a cover, but for this author economising on tyres, brake linings or steering head bearings has always seemed plain stupid. Renewing the inner tubes of any recently-acquired, second-hand machine is also strongly advised.

Now we shall look at the things you will definitely need — the First Line — followed by the desirable but non-essential items — the Second Line — and finish up with the boring but necessary documentation — insurance, plus the club membership to get it economically, an MOT, and a V5 log book. Cost of road tax (£20-£40 a year, according to engine size), a licence (£17 for full or provisional at present), or training and the Test (today £35 minimum plus £16.50 respectively) have not been included, so take them into account if they affect you. Finally, there is a brief section on shopping.

As a cheerful preliminary, it's worth itemising useful things that you can probably get from your immediate environment, including from your B & C auxiliaries, without expenditure. First is the **Big Box** — preferably a wooden tea chest, but a really sturdy cardboard box lined with plastic bags will do at a pinch. Into this goes everything you discard from the bike — never throw anything away, as it is amazing how either other people or yourself later with another machine, find a use for almost everything. Organised in plastic bags and labelled with tie-on luggage labels, at the very least the things can be produced to show what you want to renew.

Other and potentially useful free stuff includes:

Empty coffee tins and jam jars for storing nuts, bolts, etc.

Plastic bags including clear ones.

Rags, especially cotton ones for cleaning.

3-in-one oil — there's usually some about — for lubricating cables, etc.

Any tools you can scrounge.

Wire — both as metal string and, and if it's the correct type, for electrical emergencies.

Old tobacco tins, for keeping spares and especially bulbs in a secure, compact and portable container which you can then label with their contents.

A good padlock (if you're lucky).

Old tyre inner tube, and sections of foam rubber — the former for 'rubber mounting' components, the latter for cushioning the battery.

A cover, and a plastic groundsheet — see Section I.

A suitable plastic 'wallet' or roll, for carrying your tools in.

'Home-made hand cleaner' — i.e. washing-up liquid mixed with any abrasive scouring powder like *Ajax*. Use it if it's there, and save on *Swarfega*.

A hard plastic shopping or sports bag, preferably dark coloured — this is an important item. It should be big enough to take your helmet, etc., but compact enough to fasten to the back of your seat with bungies. You may have to buy one, but sports bags do hang about most households. You can even embellish them with reflective tape for conspicuity. Then you have something to carry your tools and chain/lock in as you ride, and your helmet and overtrousers when you leave the bike secured. This does away with leaving tools and spares unsecured on the bike behind unlockable panels. And means that you don't have to fit a top-heavy, expensive and unsightly top-box to leave your helmet in. Your right arm may get a bit longer from the weight of your bag, but if you find a nice-looking one, you shouldn't lose too many penalty points socially.

And so to

The First Line

A small notebook — compact enough to carry in a riding jacket pocket, this cheap and apparently insignificant item is highly useful. In it keep a record of purchase dates, and mileages of services and replacements, with their costs. It adds up to a living record of your involvement with the machine, and lets you know when things are coming due for renewal — you may think you'll never forget when you had to spend the £70 on new tyres, but with the mileage recorded you'll know how long ago it was for sure. (Keep the bills as well, though, to impress people when you come to sell.) Tyre pressures, engine and frame numbers, oil mixture and types, ignition and lock key numbers, etc., all go in the notebook.

40p

A suitable handbook and parts book — for the first, either the factory riders' manual, or a Pitmans or Pearson handbook — originals of these can all be found at £3 to £4 at major autojumbles. Or photocopies of the factory handbooks can usually also be had from Bruce Main-Smith. These 129 little books provide you with essential information — the rest will be discussed in **The SecondLine**. The parts book is crucial; it will show you what should be there, what it looks like, and how it fits together, plus telling you what an item is called so you can order a new one.   **£6-£8.00**

Tools — the necessary two or three open-ended or ring spanners, a double-ended screwdriver (Philips and cheesehead), a good 9 inch adjustable spanner, a spark plug spanner, feeler gauges, pliers and insulating or duct tape. If you are starting from scratch, this is the get-you-home kit. Go round the bike to find what spanners you need to remove the petrol tank, wheels, etc., and where the adjustable spanner will serve instead. For the latter, it is worth spending out on a good one. The rest can sometimes be found economically at autojumbles and second-hand tool shops (for which see *Yellow Pages*). Things should be accumulated gradually when a definite need arises, but you will need these ones for your tool roll from the start.   **£22.00**

Spares — cables (clutch, front brake, and throttle, plus air lever and back brake as necessary, £10), bulbs (front, rear and pilot, £4), a couple of spark plugs (£3). Again, these are the basic get-you-home minimum. Even the air and throttle cables will probably duplicate one another. Some people carry their spare cables rolled up inside the headlamp, and sometimes have their bulbs taped in there too, but this does clutter up an already confined space which is subject to damp and vibration. Likewise rockers used to carry their spare chain links attached to the zippers of their leather jackets, but metal can quickly wear through our preferred material, waxed cotton. Label the cables for an easier time by the roadside.   **£20.50**

Helmet and goggles/visor — for British lightweight speeds an open-face helmet is acceptable and looks the part — it's hard to come on like Darth Vader in a full-face helmet on a Francis-Barnett. A white helmet is an easy and genuine aid to conspicuity. All helmets must carry the appropriate British Standards kite mark. Get the best you can afford, from a shop where you can try it on, rather than by mail order; a good fit is literally vital, so it may feel a little tight at first and may need easing apart slightly to get on. Eye protection is equally vital. Traditional glass Mk VIII etc. goggles for about £18 are good unless you wear glasses; some Scott plastic goggles will fit over spectacles with a little loss of peripheral vision. Otherwise a visor at around £15 (only the Bob Heath Jet Flip one is legal at present) is a very acceptable alternative.   **£35.00-£50.00**

Gloves — once again, it's worth some expense and care in choosing here. Purpose-built motorcycle gloves will wear longest, protect your hands in a fall, and (especially the modern ones) keep out the worst of the wet and cold. Buy black gloves which are wide enough at their open end to fit over the sleeves of your jacket. A pair of dark silk inner gloves can be added for £2 or £3, both for extra warmth and to put on and protect the gloves' inside after you have got your hands dirty tinkering at the

roadside.   **£15.00-£25.00**

These D1-mounted ladies look seriously well-equipped for jaunting, though in the early fifties you could get away with a flying helmet. Glad to see they joined the RAC, though.

Jacket — the single most important element of your wardrobe, and experience says there's only one choice. A leather jacket may be ideal for skin protection and tough posing (though the latter is hard to sustain on a Bantam), and a *Rukka* or similar suit for water-proofing. But leather isn't particularly warm or waterproof, synthetic waterproof suits are not that hardy, and for a decent example each costs up to £100.00. The all-round and economical answer is a black waxed cotton jacket. This is purpose-built (look at the neck and pockets), almost fully waterproof, renewable (you wax it every winter), and repairable (you can buy repair kits with patches and waxed thread). The wax/dirt does rub off, but not very much once the garment is worn in. You want the thigh-length type, belted at the waist with four outside pockets. *Barbour* and *Belstaff* in that order (Barbour give you an inside pocket as well) are the big names here, and sometimes can be found on offer or as seconds for around our price. Otherwise, several outlets offer acceptable budget versions of their own. Check the length — shorter may look better but not cover your lower back and bottom when you're seated in a riding position — and the fit and fastening of the 131

high collar, which should have a buckle you can do up and undo with gauntleted hands. The neck's good fit, reinforced with a scarf (rockers sometimes used to favour nappies, for their moisture absorbent qualities) is a big element in the waterproofing, and the reason why using the green country gents version with a conventional collar which you may already own, isn't really on for regular riding. If you remember to wrap up sharp objects (like a screwdriver), your jacket's capacious pockets will carry most of what you need (spare keys, your notebook in a little plastic bag, a rag for your hands, your spare link, bungies, maps, and maybe a Swiss Army knife, or a multi-tool like the Leather-man Survival Tool which includes screwdriver, file, and pliers, etc.). Also the garment is socially at least neutral. Modern variants come with built-in quilted linings, but I prefer the *'Trialmaster'* type, a plain waxed cotton shell, with detachable linings and sweaters, etc,. then worn underneath for warmth as required; that way you can still use the jacket itself comfortably in hot weather. This design basically has not changed in over 40 years, and the reason is because it's right.
£45.00

Overtrousers — here you can economise a little, as you will not wear overtrousers anything like as often as you do the jacket, so a cheap pair of heavy black or yellow PVC ones (not treated nylon) from Millets or similar, is OK to start with. Make sure they are long enough with your knees bent in the riding position, and preferably that the trouser bottoms can be secured tightly enough with poppers or Velcro. If the need justifies it, and when you can afford them, waxed cotton trousers have all the jacket's virtues and are also quite warm.
£10.00

Boots — boots may seem a bit over the top with a lightweight, but most accidents involve damage to the feet and legs, and even with a low speed tumble, metal and hot exhaust pipes on the feet and ankles can be nasty. *Derri boots* are economical, warm and totally waterproof but like Wellingtons, offer only a limited protection. Full-dress motorcycle boots are pricier, and are usually worn conspicuously outside your trousers. The best compromise is black leather lace-up boots around 9in high, with sewn-in tongues for waterproofing, and thick socks, or two pairs of thinner wool ones, taking care of the cold. *Doctor Martins* are OK at around £25.00, but in most cities a good budget option exists in the form of industrial footwear, which will have all the above features plus welded-on soles and probably steel toecaps, another useful safety edge. Look in the *Yellow Pages* for 'Footwear Manufacturers' or 'Footwear Wholesalers' to locate a pair. Be careful, however, that the shape of the boots' toe is reasonably slim rather than so bulbous that it will make gear changing awkward. Waterproof your boots with *Nik-Wax* or *Wet-Pruf* polish, and you will have tough practical footwear, inconspicuous under your trousers, which should also be comfortable to walk around in.
£15.00-£25.00

Padlock and chain — see p22 A shackle lock is ideal but more expensive, so a good brass-bodied padlock and a length of chain either from the ironmonger or, if you can afford it, plastic coated from the bike shop, is the heavy but economical answer. **£6.00-£10.00**

The bag — another important item. The initial choice (panniers are Second Line) is between a kit-bag with shoulder straps, and a black plastic sports/shopping bag. It should be big enough to take: overtrousers, bottle of two-stroke oil, lock and chain, aerosol of *Finilec* puncture repair, tool roll and helmet. That way you are fully mobile at both ends of your journey. The bag is then bungied to your pillion seat. If you regularly carry a pillion passenger, he or she must be prepared to wear the sack on their shoulders, or preferably you will have to fit a luggage rack. Modern racks can often be adapted to suit, or you may find a suitably old one at an autojumble. **£6.00-£10.00**

Bungies — absolutely vital kit, these elasticated cords with hooks at each end. Carry at least four, in two different lengths, and make sure that the plastic coating on the hooks extends all the way over their ends, to help prevent scraping your paintwork. Have a care securing them, as they can snap back viciously. **£3.00**

A mirror — a mirror seems to me an absolutely necessary part of riding. Fixing the kind that come on stems clamped to the handlebars so that they don't blow out of position is a fine and frustrating art. The answer is the kind of mirror with a fixture that goes in the end of the handlebars. Modern bar-end ones look fine, and are half the price of the reproduction old style chrome jobs. **£10.00**

Rescue service membership — die-hards will say this is a frivolity and one that indicates Lack of Moral Fibre — that you should be able to fix your own machine. This is little consolation late at night by the side of the motorway, on a long bridge or in a tunnel, when the big ends have let go, and the call-out fee for rescue is more than a year's membership. You may have a spouse/mate/parent with a pick-up or trailer who is willing to turn out for you at all hours, but even these paragons do sometimes go on holiday, etc., and inevitably that is when disaster strikes. Riding old bikes is, after all, supposed to be fun, and I feel that the peace of mind a rescue back-up brings is part of that. The principal services on offer are the *AA* or the *RAC*. Both are good — over the years the *RAC* guys have turned out for me at one or two moments of distress, and never been less than helpful and sympathetic (see p.141). The *AA* has a larger organisation, and at the time of writing (1989) the cost of their Riders Club membership (£27.50 if you pay by direct debit) including the Relay Recovery Service, which gets you, your passenger and machine to any single destination in the UK, is lower than the opposition. But check with each for current rates and services offered before making a decision. If you already hold personal membership of either organisation, it covers you for your bike (any number of vehicles with the *AA*, up to three with the *RAC*.) **£27.50**

Total   low   **£220.90**
                             high   **£265.90** 133

Rain or shine, a waxed cotton jacket is the best all-rounder.

Juggle the high and low total, minus whatever items you have already, with the cost of the bike itself plus immediate work and replacements, the insurance (currently, for an over 25 year old, £51 fully comp. with the VMCC schemes subject to status) and if necessary an MOT (currently £7.92), and bingo, there's your more or less £500 on the road.

The Second Line

That's not all, though; it never is. So here are some more items, non-essential but highly desirable.

More books — knowing about your machine is not just a matter of pride, it can help you understand, improve and advantageously replace parts on it. As a motorcycle author myself, the following is going to sound a little like Abbie Hoffman's 60s title *Steal This Book,* but — it's not really necessary to buy everything available. Your local library may have some of the marque histories and manuals and may be able to get others, and your fellow Club members should be able to lend you some. Roy Bacon's Collectors' Library series for Osprey cover the ground and have very useful data tables at the back. The same goes for his big BSA Singles Restoration book which includes Bantams. His general Restoration series is quite useful, but probably not enough to justify buying. In the restoration line, two titles are worth looking for. **The Vintage Motorcyclists' Workshop** by Radco of the VMCC is a likeable work, full of useful hints. And if full restoration becomes your aim, then **The Restoration of Vintage and Thoroughbred Motorcycles** by Jeff Clew is well worth a look. Both are published by Haynes.

For an original workshop manual, either your Club, autojumbles, or the specialist second-hand book dealers listed in **Classic Bike's parts and Services Guide** are likely sources. Bruce Main-Smith, for reproduced manuals and parts books, has already been mentioned. If you want original contemporary material on your machine, a visit to the British Periodical Library opposite the Underground station at Colindale in north London (Tel. 01-200 5515) will yield bound and indexed volumes of **The Motor Cycle** and **Motor Cycling,** and the staff will photocopy any road tests, etc., which you require, for a nominal charge. The National Motorcycle Museum outside Birmingham (Tel. 06755 3311) intends offering similar services, and the National Motor Museum at Beaulieu, Hants. (Tel. 0590 612123) does so too; ring them for details. **Classic Bike** offer a similar service for a price, but you may find that your Club do it for next to nothing.

More tools — bit by bit, more spanners, a hacksaw, a file, maybe a socket set, a small grease gun, electrical wire and a bulb for fault tracing, emery paper for the points, spare nuts and bolts, etc.

Tyre stuff — *Finilec,* an aerosol which inflates a punctured inner tube, and if the puncture is a small one, seals it for a while, hopefully to get you somewhere you can replace it. Buy the large size. If you're going touring, a puncture kit, spare inner tube, tyre levers and a pump.

A battery charger — one that does both 6- and 12-volt batteries. Use the trickle charge only, overnight. For around £10.00 it can make cold mornings a lot easier. A bottle of distilled water and an eye dropper for topping up the battery, plus Vaseline to waterproof the battery terminals.

Better gear — bit by bit again, as and when you feel the need justifies it. Waxed cotton overtrews. Throw-over panniers — *Swagman* are good. A proper canvas cover for the bike if it lives out, and a *Kryptonite-* type lock. A pencil torch for one of your jacket pockets, the *Mity-Lite* is excellent. And so on.

Paperwork

Details of applying for a driving licence and road tax for the vehicle can be found on leaflets from the Post Office, and likewise on training and taking a driving test (leaflet D100 at the time of writing). Insurance has already been mentioned. If your machine needs an MOT, Club members should be able to tell you the nearest testing station garage with a sympathetic attitude to older machinery.

The largest bureaucratic hassle likely to be encountered is if you have bought a machine without a V5 registration document. If it has had one and it has been lost, Swansea should replace it on application. But if it was not issued with one before the records were closed in 1983 (see p.18), you will have to make sure that a new and appropriate, 'age-related' registration number is issued for your machine. If it is a pre-'63 motorcycle that means a three-letter, three-number registration. Otherwise you will want an appropriate suffix number, the same as the one on the machine's old registration. If the number plate is missing and the old registration is not known, in most cases you can date the machine by means of its engine and frame numbers from the tables in this or other books, from Club records, or by applying to **Classic Bike** who charge £10 for the service, 135 or **British Bike Magazine** who, at the time of writing, do it for nothing. The relevant appropriate registration suffixes go like this:

A   February 1963—December 1963
B   January 1964—December 1964
C   January 1965—December 1965
D   January 1966—December 1966
E   January 1967—July 1967
F   August 1967—July 1968
G   August 1968—July 1969
H   August 1969—July 1970
J   August 1970—July 1971

Getting an age-related number should present no great difficulty if you are methodical. The machine should be roadworthy and ready for its MOT. Contact your nearest Local Vehicle Licensing Office (LVLO). They will give you a form to complete, and send someone round to look at the bike and check its engine and frame numbers. You should then arrange a letter for the LVLO confirming the vehicle's age and authenticity. This letter should come from your Club historian, or any other acknowledged experts, such as the staff of one of the classic magazines. The more official the notepaper and language, the better. The letter is essential, but after that the LVLO should issue you with an age-related number within a couple of weeks. An original registration number, incidentally, is usually only reissued to a machine of special interest or one with a certifiable place in motorway history, like a racer, which none of our mass-produced lightweights are likely to be, but see **STOP PRESS** on p.20.

Shopping

If you live in one of the urban centres in the South or the Midlands which is blessed with a British bike shop, you are lucky, and should cultivate it. The best way to do this is buy things there, every time you go in, even if it's only a plug or a tube of chrome cleaner. Consider buying your tyres and battery there, even though you could get them cheaper by mail order., You are supporting something useful and building a relationship. Helpful advice and information from the people in the know should come of this, but don't expect it as a right, and only ask for it at times when the shop staff are not busy.

Getting work done on a British bike is a subject in itself. Your Club is, once again, your best guide. The British bike shop may do it, or know a man who will. An all-purpose motorcycle shop, the smaller the better, should do general work such as seal renewal, rebores, wheel building, etc., though they may not touch older bikes at all. Personal contacts are the best way. A good rule, rather than asking vaguely that your machine be "made well", is to determine one or two specific problem areas. That way you are more likely to be able to get an estimate on the work in terms of both time and cost. Try to get a written estimate, ideally signed by the shop/engineer. But realistically allow about a third more on cost quoted, and on the time! Some jobs can be contracted out to specialists by post, and a list of them will be found at the end of this chapter.

If you live outside the South or the Midlands, you will probably also have to buy your parts by mail order. A few basic procedures can help here. First, sit down and make a list of what you need; include as much as possible, as in some cases, the larger the order, the less postage. Get the names and numbers of the bits from your parts book; the shop may not find the part numbers relevant, but it will let them know you are concentrating. Top the list with the make, type, year and engine number of your machine.

Next ring the shop briefly to make sure it still exists. This is not a frivolous procedure. It can save a wasted journey or letter. Many suppliers are essentially one-man or one-family businesses. Sometimes they close for holidays, sometimes they just close.

If you can afford it, and the time seems right for the shop person (i.e. they're not busy) tell them on the phone what you need. If they quote you prices, ask whether these include VAT. If your list is long, read it off to them and arrange to ring back in an hour or two after they have checked their stock; this saves a long wait with your phone bill growing the while. If you want some information or a discussion about a bike problem with them, it is only polite to first ask if it is a convenient time for them to talk; and to remember that the object is to find out what they know, rather than show off what you do.

But normally, once you know they're there, send them the list plus an s.a.e. The list should be typed or written in block capitals, with one item per line and a space left on the right for a price. Shops like C & D handle a great volume of mail order business, and you owe it to them to make things as smooth as possible. It's also always worth asking if the shops do a discount for your Owners Club, and, if relevant, whether you can pay by credit card. They will send back the list indicating what is available and its price including p & p plus VAT. You can often pay by plastic (Access, Visa), or otherwise with a cheque or postal order; sometimes you can arrange to pay COD (cash on delivery). If items arrive damaged or the order is incomplete, write to the shop promptly, quoting the order and invoice numbers. You should be credited with the difference as well as any postage costs. Over many years, I have never found a British bike mail order firm that was anything but friendly and honest, but if you have a problem, contact your local Citizens' Advice Bureau.

To save the cost of postage and to shop around for second-hand cycle parts (or even a derelict machine or basket case the same as your own bike, to cannibalise for spares) visit an autojumble. Ones within easy reach of where you live are always worth a look. Otherwise the two big annual events are the Classic Bike Show organised in the Midlands by Alan Whitehead, and the big Autumn autojumble at Beaulieu. If you're going to the latter, take full waterproof gear, as it never fails to pour!

Useful information

Insurance: Carole Nash, VMCC and certain one-make club schemes, 19 Mayfield Road, Timperley, Altrincham, Cheshire WA15 7TB (Tel. 061-980 1305).

Tyres: Classic Tyres, 8 Willow Way, Coalpit Heath, Bristol BS17 2SG (Tel. 0454 774903).
Armour Motor Products Ltd., 784 Wimborne Road, Moordown, Bournemouth, Dorset BH9 2HS (Tel. 0202 419409) for Chen Shing tyres.

Wheelbuilding: The Central Wheel Co., Lichfield Road, Water Orton, Birmingham B46 1NU (Tel. 021-747 5175).
Alf Hagon, 350 – 352 High Road, Leyton, London E10 (Tel. 01-539 8146/01-556 9200).

Electrical: M.C.E. Services, Unit 10, Ladbrook Park Industrial Estate, Miller's Road, Warwick, CV34 5AJ (Tel. 0926 499756). Wiring Harnesses.
Merv Plastics (CB), 201 Station Road, Beeston, Notts. NG9 2AB (Tel. 0602 222783) Electrical components.
Armours (see Tyres) Harnesses, switches, components, etc.

Carburettors: IMI Amal Ltd., Holdford Road, Wilton, Birmingham B6 7OS (Tel. 021-356 2000). Will advise on and supply suitable Concentric replacements, jetting, etc.
Avon Engineering, Manse Brae, Avonbridge, Falkirk FK1 2LU (Tel. 032486 574) Reconditioning Concentric or Monobloc.
DMW (see p.111) Villiers carburettor spares.

Suspension Units: Russler Racing, Mackadown Lane, Kitts Green, Birmingham B33 0LQ (Tel. 021-784 8266). Rebuilds for Girling adjustable units.
Alf Hagon (see Wheelbuilding). Will advise on suitable replacement units.

Seats: R.K. Leighton, Unit 6, Gunsmith House, 50-54 Price Street, Birmingham B4 6JZ (Tel. 021-359 0514). Re-covering and rebuilding.

Cables: Armours (see Tyres).

Exhausts and silencers: Armours (see Tyres).

Nuts, bolts, etc.: CDS Accessories, 57 High Street, Dartford, Kent (Tel. 0322 77484).

Transfers: VMCC Transfer Scheme, 'Arosfa', Cwmpennar, Mountain Ash, Mid-Glamorgan CF45 3DL. Will advise, and supply complete sets for most old machines.

Chapter Twelve
True story

Having ploughed through the foregoing welter of yawn-inducing technical stuff and soporifically sensible good advice, the management's policy is that you have now earned a little light relief. This takes the form of a first-hand account of a couple of British lightweights out on The Road. We hope you will be joining them shortly. As demonstrated by the story, which involves the author, these motorcycles are **practically** foolproof . . .

Two go mad on the Mynd

One September a few years ago I and my friend Richard Howard, the actor, decided to take a long Bantam-break weekend. Richard, like me, was in his mid-30s, had recently returned to biking and was now well on the learning curve with a nice red B175. I had been part-time despatch riding in London, also on a B175, a blue one with some D14/4 Sports bits tacked on (Sports seat, mudguards, full-width hubs, etc.).

It was decided that a shakedown run for Richard's bike could be combined with a couple of nights under canvas on the only kind of campsite worth bothering about — a farmer's field, in Shropshire, beneath the spectacularly beautiful Long Mynd, a hill shaped like an upturned boat four miles long. The Mynd presents a sheer enough face westwards to the Welsh marches to have encouraged both a glider club, whose airfield sits on top of it, and hang gliders, who don't always get along with the glider folk.

Surrounded by fine walking in quiet countryside dotted sparsely with some good country pubs, in my judgement the Mynd was Bantam Country. The final attraction was that it was within reach for another friend of mine, a tall, red-headed person of the female persuasion, whose work in fashion was Midlands based, and who was happily free to join us on the Saturday.

So I dug out the *Blacks Good Companion* tent, the black leatherette bicycle saddlebags, an old army knapsack and a Girl Scout's rucksack;

Street-wise. The author's B175, with D14/4 Sports bits, ready for the off to the Mynd.

the Bantams lacked racks, so we carried our sleeping bags on our shoulders, and the rest in rolls and the saddle-bags, arrangements which proved quite OK. The plan was to leave London the first day and, as far as possible by A-roads, ride to Bristol where a friend was to lend us a flat for the night. I had spares, bulbs, cables and so on for my working bike, but since we would be sharing them I checked them over, and found no throttle cable, and no spare link for the rear chain. Rich wasn't bothered, but being a list-maker, the evening before we left I managed to get these items at my local bike shop in the Essex Road in Islington.

We set out in reasonably good order on a sunny Thursday morning. I was glad of my bar-end mirror for keeping track of a sometimes hesitant Richard in the remains of the rush-hour traffic. In the shadow of the Westway we followed the A4 out to Heathrow Airport, and only joined the M4 motorway at exit 5. We got off again at exit 8/9, but even that was enough motorway. 'I didn't like that,' said Richard succinctly when we stopped, and though I thought the Bantams had done all right, droning along at 50 in line aport to discourage people from cutting us up, the way the backlash from trucks and coaches tried to shove the little bikes off line did take some getting used to. As planned, we stayed off motorways from then until the return journey.

The weather was good and the morning's ride increasingly delightful as we crossed the Thames at Henley, turned off for Abingdon and cut through, past the old MG works, to Kingston Bagpuize and the A420, the Oxford to Swindon road that had been the main artery of my formative years. It was good, riding along in the sunshine between the familiar fields, with the low bulk of the Berkshire Downs and the Uffington White Horse rising off to the left; and at lunchtime when we turned off a few miles short of Faringdon, the pub was still there where I remembered it.

We ate, drank and moved on out, and I was nearly at the crossroads before I realised that I was alone. As Richard had driven out from the car park, his throttle cable had snapped. Not to worry, I carolled, and with a flourish produced the cable purchased with such foresight the previous day. But when we had removed his carburettor and were fitting the new cable, disaster struck. The throttle spring, compressed for refastening, slipped from oily fingers, and with one bound was over the hedge and free. Prolonged, meticulous searching in the field never did discover it.

I rode into Faringdon, but the old bicycle shop had gone and the Eagle Garage was more interested in selling soft drinks than spares. So I rode back and we called the RAC. And here the Magic of the Bantam came into play. The RAC man was large and local, and frankly admitted that if the bike had been Japanese he would have shoved it in the back of his van and let a shop sort it out if it could. But since it was a good old British Bantam, he found a roughly suitable spring among his spares, pulled, stretched, cut it to length and fitted it, and this arrangement not only worked but continued to do so until Richard sold the bike over a year later.

We proceeded gratefully but briskly, for there were 70 miles or so to cover and half the afternoon was gone. We negotiated Swindon, crossed the M4 at junction 16, and followed the A420 into Chippenham. A little saddle sore, we stopped at a garage there for petrol and a soft drink, and it was one of those moments - two-strokes, Cola, hanging around a garage in the soft light of a late Wiltshire afternoon, and my youth came flooding back. Then it was on to Bristol.

Next morning as we were loading up, the pair of little bikes looked so well against the railings that someone took a picture. Bristol was Richard's patch, so we breakfasted like champions in the Blackboy Cafe at the top of Whiteladies Road, before taking the back way to the Severn Bridge and whirring over it, feeling the wind's shove from the cloudy water far below. Round Chepstow, toiling up a steep, forested hill, and then coasting down the other side, briefly regretting the absence of faster, better-handling machines as the twisting hillside road revealed below to the right the first glimpses of the River Wye and the glorious ruins of Tintern Abbey. A pint in a cold stone pub, and by early afternoon we had followed the A49 along the line of border towns, Ross, Hereford, Leominster and Ludlow, and turned off left down the A489, skirting the southern stern of the Mynd's upturned boat before turning right down the lanes along its western side. Eventually, we bumped into the farmer's field at Ratlinghope, just 101 miles from our Bristol start.

The weather had turned, and we pitched the tent by an old oak at the top of the sloping field and got busy with the camping Gaz, a tin of Irish stew, and the Krackawheat biscuits. With the Bantams resting at angles with bits of wood under their propstands, we huddled out of the wind in the orange tent, lying on the lofting sleeping bags, groaning a bit, but savouring the romance of the mess-tins and the line of the hills all round, and eyeing the only two fellow campers. By coincidence, these were also a pair of bikers, our dwarf alter egos, youngsters on small DT Yamahas. At first the two parties studiously ignored each other, but later that night inevitably we got acquainted in a pub which was a walkable mile away. These young lads were the self-styled Hermits from Knutsford, so named in a spirit of satire because of the reclusive, obscure nature of their tenuous club. But they were all right with me, as they had actually read one of my novels, and also seemed to have liked it (thereby putting themselves **141** into a further minority). At closing time we tottered back to the field and parted with mutual expressions of esteem.

We had warm sleeping bags, polonecks, and a good deal of drink taken, but it was a cold night, the ground was hard, and despite some long hours in the saddle, sleep proved elusive. Finally, in the hours after dawn, with the plaintive bleating of sheep echoing from the hills around, a brief deep sleep came. But then it was interrupted by one of the Hermits, who announced from outside the tent that they had rolled a wake-up herbal cigarette, and would we care to join them? This kindly-meant offer was rejected with a joint bellow of incipient middle age as Richard and I both, groaning, tried to regain that oasis of beautiful slumber.

The author (right) and his Thespian companion Richard Howard, about to board their Bantams in Bristol and head for the hills.

After a breakfast of Alpen in our mugs, we tottered off to walk the surrounding hills for a bit. It was a nice morning, soft and with only a breeze, and we would have made fair progress up the lanes had it not been for Richard's habit, echoing a tendency to hang back on the bike, of stopping when he had something to say. Often these pauses concerned his lovely girlfriend Mary, whom he was missing.

My own red-headed friend turned up at the site after lunch, and in improbably fashion-conscious heels, wobbled up the Mynd with us. Along the top, lying by their Volvo like surfers waiting for sets of waves, we found two middle-aged hang gliding men, gazing out westwards, down the steep slope and over the quiet patchwork of fields below, waiting for the wind. We got talking, the subject turned to bikes, and it turned out that one of them had owned a Sunbeam S7, and actually visited BSA's Redditch factory with a service problem, Redditch being where both the post-war Sunbeams and the Bantams had been built. We told them that at least some of the Redditch products were still performing well, and left them to the silent contemplation of the sky.

In the evening I climbed into my friend's car and with Richard riding seriously in our wake, we threaded through the lanes to the market town of Bishops Castle, where there was a pub that brewed its own beer, and a hotel. We drank the pale, caramel-coloured brew at the one and ate a good meal in the dining room of the other, our boots and riding gear being no problem as the place was used to long-distance walkers from the Offa's Dyke path.

Then Richard rode back to the camp alone. After the warm day there was mist in the lanes, and being new to the area, within a few minutes he was hopelessly lost. Under a hazy moon he pottered uncertainly between the hedgerows, finally coming to a halt beneath a signpost which informed him that he was in The Bog. (A check of the map the following day showed that an area some miles west of the Mynd did indeed bear that brief but expressive title.) Next to the signpost was a red telephone box. Dismounting, wading through the moonlit mist, Richard entered the box, telephoned his girlfriend Mary in London, told her about his situation, and enjoyed a strange, dream-like conversation.

After that he mounted the Bantam again and rode east by feel, until the Mynd bulked before him in the moonlit distance and he hit the familiar stretch of road which led him back to the silent camp. It would be nice to record that he enjoyed a sound sleep after his wanderings, but before dawn the following morning he was awakened by ominous snufflings and stampings which shook the ground he lay on. When he eventually stuck his head out of the canvas, it was to find that a brown and white cow had got into the site field.

It was ten when my friend dropped me back at the site that Sunday morning, and eleven by the time we were packed, mounted and on the road again. As we were leaving, one of the Hermits ran up waving something. It was a copy of the national magazine in which I had an article that month, and he wanted me to sign it. This was a first for me, and I was touched.

But after that the day was definitely the downside of the trip. Dogged by the back-to-school sense of returning to London and work the next day, this was the veritable wages of sin, as the journey back to London was nearly 200 miles, and having left too late, we would share the last part of it with a multitude of returning weekenders. Added to that it was a hot, sultry day, the kind where exhaust fumes hang in the air; and I was soon truly fagged by the various recent exertions and lack of sleep, and grumpy with it. The pint at lunchtime, usually a reviver, that day was just an irritating soporific. Richard, on the other hand, a man who had been known to fall asleep as abruptly as the Dormouse at the Mad Hatter's Tea Party in the middle of important movies, dinner parties or even halfway through a conversation, rode unflaggingly all day, and with no complaint.

Even the roads seemed tedious. After cutting across to Much Wenlock, they were wide, Midlands A-roads to Bridgnorth, Kidderminster, round Worcester, and on to Evesham, often dual carriageways which dwarfed the Bantams and emphasised our slow progress. By the time we got to Oxford it was late afternoon, I was in poor order, and the traffic was building nicely. We rejected the M40 and rode down through Wellingford, back to Henley — at least these were pleasant and familiar roads — and then, as the dusk deepened, back on to the M4 at Exit 8/9.

We were doing all right, with the 'last leg' feeling to sustain us in the heavy traffic, when there was a terrific metal 'whang' from my bike and all power was gone. I declutched instinctively and coasted in fast to the **143** hard shoulder. My rear chain's spring link had broken, and only good fortune had prevented the chain wrapping around the wheel or jamming in the engine and seizing the rear wheel.

I produced the newly-purchased spare link with satisfaction, but once again that was only the beginning. As the traffic howled and whined past I rethreaded the chain and when the two open ends were next to each other on the lower run, locked the machine in gear. Then we tried to stretch the ends close enough together to insert the new link. As full darkness came on, we tugged and struggled with our bare hands, screwdrivers, pliers, desperately trying to gain that fraction of an inch that would allow the connection to be made. We loosened off the chain adjusters all the way, feverishly counting turns each side, but still no joy.It was a quarter of an hour but seemed a great deal longer before almost casually I tried putting the Bantam into neutral, the clutch wheel spun freely and the chain ends finally joined. There's no fool like an old fool, drunk with exhaustion, at the side of the M4 on a Sunday night, and that's for sure.

Riding on in the full dark with filthy hands, we soon turned off the beastly motorway again at Exit 5, and after the roundabout under the Chiswick flyover, riding in a maze of last gasp concentration, Richard led us through the west London streets where he had grown up to Shepherds Bush, where I took over and took us through Notting Hill and Westbourne Grove. We refuelled there, then crossed the Edgware Road and rode north up through Camden Town, the back way to Islington and finally, home.

Some time after that, an incredibly boring intellectual English film called *Radio On* was released, in which the post-existential hero declared portentously that 'It's still possible to make a journey' as he drove an old Rover 100 agonisingly slowly from London to Bristol. Richard and I had

a good laugh at that. We knew that with the Bantams it was indeed possible to 'make a journey', have mild adventures and a good time too. If the little machines haven't featured largely in this account, it's because they did what they were asked to do without fuss, and the only things that broke on them could be fixed. Is that practical, or what?

And so we say farewell. After a final word on the emergency start procedure, its youthful new keeper rode my last B175 Bantam off into the sunset. With my helmet.